2022

Inside Wikipedia

Inside Wikipedia

How It Works and
How You Can Be an Editor

Paul A. Thomas

ROWMAN & LITTLEFIELD
Lanham • Boulder • New York • London

Published by Rowman & Littlefield
An imprint of The Rowman & Littlefield Publishing Group, Inc.
4501 Forbes Boulevard, Suite 200, Lanham, Maryland 20706
www.rowman.com

86-90 Paul Street, London EC2A 4NE

British Library Cataloguing in Publication Information Available

Library of Congress Cataloging-in-Publication Data

Names: Thomas, Paul A. (Paul Anthony), author.
Title: Inside Wikipedia : how it works and how you can be an editor / Paul A. Thomas.
Description: Lanham : Rowman & Littlefield Publishers, [2022] | Includes
   bibliographical references and index.
Identifiers: LCCN 2022014021 (print) | LCCN 2022014022 (ebook) | ISBN
   9781538163214 (cloth) | ISBN 9781538163221 (ebook)
Subjects: LCSH: Wikipedia—Handbooks, manuals, etc. | Wikipedia. | Authorship—
   Collaboration. | Electronic encyclopedias.
Classification: LCC AE100 .T527 2022 (print) | LCC AE100 (ebook) | DDC 030—
   dc23/eng/20220323
LC record available at https://lccn.loc.gov/2022014021
LC ebook record available at https://lccn.loc.gov/2022014022

Contents

Acknowledgments

Writing this book would not have been possible without help from the following individuals: LiAnna Davis of the Wiki Education Foundation; Charles Harmon and Erinn Slanina at Rowman & Littlefield; Dr. Emily Vardell, Dr. Sarah Sutton, Dr. Ludi Price, Dr. Michael Widdersheim at Emporia State's School of Library and Information Management; and Carmen Orth-Alfie, Karna Younger, Tami Albin, Josh Bolick, Marianne Reed, Natalie Mahan, Brian Moss, Wendi Arant Kaspar, and Burkley Hermann. Special thanks also go to the millions of editors who have made Wikipedia such a massive place.

Here, have a barnstar!

Introduction

When I was about ten years old, my grandparents bought me an old copy of the *Encyclopaedia Britannica* that they had found for cheap at an estate sale. Having been published in 1973, my set was somewhat beat up, and its pages were thin and dusty, but I loved those books all the same. The volumes, with their classy, black binding and gold-tinged pages, rested on a dedicated shelf next to my bed, and many of my childhood afternoons were spent poring over entries about topics as disparate as medieval Japanese history, the circulatory system, and the geopolitics of the twentieth century. (So attached was I to my encyclopedia set that when I would get into trouble, my parents would often threaten to take away my *Britannicas*. Thankfully, this never came to pass.)

I loved (and still love) my *Britannicas*, but two issues with the encyclopedia always bothered me, even as a child.

First, my *Britannica* set was decades older than me, and as such it was noticeably out of date. (As a child interested in geography, this fact was made most apparent to me whenever I chanced upon one of the encyclopedia's maps that listed long-nonexistent states such as Czechoslovakia, a fractured Germany, Yugoslavia, and, of course, the USSR.) Unfortunately, that is the nature of printed material; as soon as you put the ink to the page, the content is already dated, irrevocably trapped in the past.

The second issue I had with my *Britannica* set was that it was woefully small. The world we live in is enormous, and humanity has spent the better part of the past ten thousand years attempting to systematically describe and classify this massive world in thousands upon thousands of books, articles, films, and other assorted media texts. In no way could any encyclopedia cram all the information we have about our reality into just twenty-four volumes. To even attempt such a feat meant that certain knowledge had to be left behind—and my *Britannica* set was proof positive that this is exactly what happened. For me, nothing was more exasperating than cracking open a volume only to discover that it lacked an article about a topic in which I was currently interested.

But then, in 2003 when I was eleven, everything changed, for this was the year that my mom introduced me to Wikipedia. "It's a free, online encyclopedia that lets *anyone* edit it," she said, her voice hinting that she was more than a bit skeptical about the idea. Of course, I had to investigate, and so I queued up Wikipedia and did a quick search for the one thing that at the time occupied most of my thoughts: *Star Wars*. When the results loaded, and I saw page after page of freely accessible articles detailing the movies, their production, and the franchise's elaborate mythology, my mind was thoroughly blown. But because I had heard that anyone could add content to the site, I was aware that Wikipedia might contain misinformation. I thus did some rudimentary fact-checking (which, as an eleven-year-old, meant comparing what was on Wikipedia with what my well-worn copy of the *Star Wars Visual Dictionary* had to say), and I was pleasantly surprised to discover that most of the site's content seemed accurate.

Although the free and expansive nature of Wikipedia was exhilarating, the thing that excited me the most about the site was its edit feature. This capability ensured that articles could be updated whenever new information was released to the public. And because the site was not a printed resource, it did not have the size limitations of physical encyclopedias; Wikipedia, it seemed, offered solutions to the problems that I had had with my *Encyclopaedia Britannica* set.

In the years immediately following my introduction to the resource, Wikipedia became one of my favorite websites to visit, but fearing that I would ruin its content, I refrained from making substantial edits, choosing instead to fix the occasional typo. This reluctance lasted until sometime in 2007, when I bit the bullet and signed up for an account (choosing, for reasons that I cannot quite remember, the ludicrous pseudonym "Gen. Quon" as my username). Soon thereafter, editing became a regular hobby of mine, and by the time I went off to college in the early- to mid-2010s, I was logging an average of around forty edits a day. As I write this introduction in the winter of 2021, I am proud to say that I have been active on the site for fifteen years and have accrued just over sixty-two thousand individual edits. Although I recognize that the site has its flaws, I nevertheless remain firm in my belief that Wikipedia is perhaps one of the most important inventions since the printing press.

In this book, I aim to share my love of Wikipedia with you by explicating in detailed but readable prose the many reasons why the site is so special, what it is that editors do, and—perhaps most important—how you can help to make the site an even better resource.

WHAT IS WIKIPEDIA?

If you have long been a heavy user of the internet, there is a good chance that you are at least somewhat familiar with Wikipedia. The "free encyclopedia that anyone can edit," Wikipedia is a noncommercial information repository—its English version alone boasts 6.3 million articles that cover everything from the biology of the human brain to the discography of "Weird Al" Yankovic. The site—a sort of digital Library of Alexandria—is a modern marvel, and every day, millions of readers flock to its many articles for information; so popular and ingrained is the site in today's world that "Wikipedia" has even become a verb (comparable to "Google"), which means "to look up information."[1]

But despite its enormous popularity, much about the site still mystifies its users. The average reader may very well know that "anyone" can edit the site, but what does this mean in practice? Who regularly edits Wikipedia? How do they do it? *Why* do they do it? In this book, I want to take a step back and consider these questions in earnest by exploring how the site functions and how you, the reader, can become a Wikipedia editor.

Having gone live in January 2001, Wikipedia is—at the time of this book's writing—well over twenty years old. A reader might reasonably ask why I have chosen to write a book at this moment, two decades after the site's digital birth. It is an understandable question, and one that has a few answers: First and foremost, many books about Wikipedia are simply old and outdated; for instance, John Broughton's *Wikipedia: The Missing Manual*—one of the more thorough surveys of the site—was published back in 2008, well over a decade ago. By covering Wikipedia's newer policies and features (such as the Visual Editor), this book serves as an important update to older works that surveyed the site.

This book was further inspired by my observation that almost every how-to book about Wikipedia is a weighty and intimidating tome containing hundreds of pages of wiki-babble. This book, in contrast, is concise and to the point, outlining editing essentials and providing illuminative anecdotes to better explain those essentials. I want this work to be user friendly and enjoyable, encouraging people of all skill levels and occupations—including librarians, educators, students, and general readers—to start working on the site.

Finally, many of the books and journal articles that survey Wikipedia do not provide an evenhanded survey of the site's strengths *and* its weaknesses; instead, some wax poetic about the site but downplay its flaws, whereas others fixate on its problems without considering any of its strengths. After reading this book, I want readers to know why Wikipedia is both a powerful resource and one that needs to be improved.

WHEN SHOULD YOU USE WIKIPEDIA?

Although this book is focused mostly on how you can become an editor and start contributing to the site, I would like to start by looking at a query to which I often find myself responding: "When is it OK to use Wikipedia?" This is a great question, but unfortunately, the answer is contextually and situationally dependent. To begin with, it is imperative to remember that Wikipedia is open to the public and that anyone can edit it. Logically, this means that when you pull information from the site, it is always possible that that info is incorrect, given that edits do not automatically go through any peer or editorial review. Because of this, I usually tell folks that Wikipedia is the perfect information source for situations in which the *stakes are low*. This means that when you get into an argument with your friend about the year that Madonna released her hit single "Vogue,"[2] or whether Jill Valentine appeared in Capcom's 2000 *Resident Evil* game *Code: Veronica*,[3] turning to Wikipedia for an answer is fine. (If, however, you are looking for practical information on bomb defusing or open-heart surgery, Wikipedia is probably not your best source.)

When it comes to academic projects, the situation becomes even more complex. In academia, you are expected to use and cite sources that have been written and peer-reviewed by experts; this ensures that you are using only the highest-quality information when crafting your own papers. Unfortunately, as I noted in the previous paragraph, Wikipedia articles, unlike many scholarly monographs and journal articles, are neither peer-reviewed (in the conventional sense) nor attributable to a single expert author. They are, instead, pseudonymous palimpsests of information written by editors who may very well not qualify as "experts" (again, in the conventional sense). Now, this does not mean that all Wikipedia articles are horrendously wrong; it simply means that Wikipedia articles in general have not been scrutinized to the same standard as scholarly sources. Indeed, for every featured article on Wikipedia written by erudite editors, many others likely either lack robust citations or are woefully incomplete.

Wikipedia's reliability is perhaps the most popular reason given for why people should avoid the site when working on academic research, but to my mind, a more compelling reason to avoid citing Wikipedia has less to do with the site's quality and more to do with its fundamental nature as a tertiary source. In the world of information literacy, a "tertiary source" refers to any resource that collects and synthesizes information originally published in other primary sources (i.e., sources that offer a firsthand account of some time period, event, or idea)[4] or secondary sources (i.e., sources that evaluate, interpret, or comment on a primary source).[5] Works such as dictionaries, encyclopedias, fact books, textbooks, guides, and thesauruses are all examples of tertiary sources, because they collect information originally published elsewhere, organizing it in a way that facilitates quick reference.

Tertiary sources are important in academia because they provide scholars with a convenient starting point for research: for instance, if you are writing about the Spanish Civil War, queuing up the *Encyclopaedia Britannica* article about the conflict will help you recognize what has already been said about the war. However, these sources are not an end in and of themselves; because these works synthesize what has been more fully discussed elsewhere, the information in tertiary sources is indirect and often abbreviated. Scholars are thus encouraged to use tertiary sources mainly as tools to locate more comprehensive primary and secondary sources. It is these sources, in turn, that you will focus most of your attention on when writing a scholarly paper, and it is these sources that you will then cite in your bibliography or works cited list.

Citing a tertiary source in a paper, on the other hand, can often signal (whether or not true) that a researcher did not do a thorough job when researching their topic.

Does all of this mean that Wikipedia is verboten at all stages of the research process? No, not at all. Instead, you merely need to use Wikipedia in an appropriate way. When I start a research project, for instance, one of the first things that I do is log onto Wikipedia and read up on the subject matter that I am interested in. But importantly, I do not stop here. Instead, I spend a considerable amount of time examining the references featured in the articles. Because these works are usually scholarly primary or secondary sources, they are exactly what I should use when I begin working on the "meat" of my paper. Put most simply, although Wikipedia should almost never be used as your *only* source for an academic project, it can often be safely used as a tool to help you find other quality books, websites, and journal articles.

GENERAL OVERVIEW OF THIS BOOK

Excepting this introduction and a conclusion, the book you are reading is divided into six main parts. In chapter 1, "The History of Wikipedia," I detail the story of how the site came to be. I first explore the millennia-old tradition of the "encyclopedia," before discussing Nupedia, an online encyclopedia cofounded by Jimmy Wales in 2000 that served as a precursor to the Wikipedia we know today. I then detail how Nupedia crashed and burned, only for Wales's next venture, Wikipedia, to emerge from the digital ashes like some sort of Web 2.0 phoenix and quickly gain in popularity. After looking at the moral panic that Wikipedia engendered with its assurance that anyone (regardless of professional credentials) could edit the site, I conclude the chapter by providing key statistical and demographic information about Wikipedia.

Chapter 2 is dedicated to what I call the "Wiki-ethos," or the overriding philosophy that (ideally) guides editors and helps them produce quality content. This ethos is fundamentally predicated on what are known as the Five Pillars of Wikipedia:

1. Wikipedia is first and foremost, an encyclopedia (i.e., it collects information for general reference use).
2. Wikipedia is neutral, citational, and never original (i.e., it is epistemologically citational and does not contain information that has not already been published elsewhere).
3. Wikipedia is free (i.e., it does not cost money for readers or editors to use it).
4. Wikipedia editors are civil to one another (i.e., Wikipedians must behave and avoid shenanigans).
5. Wikipedia is a site with no firm rules (i.e., Wikipedia has guidelines, but these can be changed given enough support).

The second part of chapter 2 comprises a list of the "dos and don'ts" of an editor. In this section—based on my own personal experiences with the site—I argue that editors should do their homework before editing, disclose any conflicts of interest, work constructively with others, and have fun when editing. Conversely, I explain why editors should avoid fighting with one another, plagiarizing content, violating copyright, or vandalizing articles.

Chapters 3 and 4 comprise step-by-step instructions detailing how one actually edits Wikipedia articles. (Of all the sections in this book, these chapters most closely resemble older works such as Broughton's *Wikipedia: The Missing Manual*.) Chapter 3 begins by exploring the basic layout of a Wikipedia article and annotating its various elements. I then walk readers through the process to create an account, and I explore why someone might want to set up such an account and what roles the various types of editors play in keeping the site in shape. I then take readers on a tour of the "User option Toolbar" before introducing them to Wikipedia's Visual Editor. (For new editors, this section may be the most interesting, given that it outlines the fastest and simplest ways to add content to articles.) Chapter 3 ends with a consideration of an article's "History" tab, which is effectively a searchable archive of every change ever made to an article.

In chapter 4, I consider more advanced editing practices by exploring the mysteries of "wikitext," or the "'behind the scenes' code"[6] used to render articles. After introducing the basics of wikitext, the chapter outlines the various ways that this code can be manually adjusted with the "wikitext editor"; this tool enables editors to eschew the Visual Editor and instead add hyperlinks, references, images, and various formatting elements to an article through direct manipulation of markup language. From here, I segue into a discussion of how editors can ensure that articles are of quality. In this portion of the chapter, I discuss the basics of Wikipedia peer review and how articles can be promoted to "good" or "featured" status. I follow this with a discussion of how certain articles can be "locked" for protection as well as how others can be deleted from Wikipedia. The chapter ends with a consideration of WikiProjects and task forces, and how they use coordination and the power of the many to improve certain content areas.

In chapter 5, I outline several approaches that editors can embrace to help improve the overall quality of the site. First, I propose that editors with a knack for grammar can help by copyediting articles. I likewise note that those interested in verifying information can improve the site by fact-checking articles. For editors who speak multiple languages, I discuss how they can translate articles from one language version of Wikipedia to another. I also detail how editors interested in media can upload images to Wikimedia Commons, allowing them to be freely used in Wikipedia articles. I then note that editors interested in accessibility can check the contrast ratios of lists and tables, or add alternative text to images. After exploring ways that interested parties can host "edit-a-thons" (or events wherein groups of people meet up, usually in person, and edit Wikipedia articles about specific topics), I conclude the chapter by discussing how Wikipedia can be integrated into education spaces such as museums, galleries, libraries, archives, and classrooms.

The book's final chapter is inspired by a 2021 essay I wrote for the *College & Research Libraries* journal titled "Reverting Hegemonic Ideology: Research Librarians and Information Professionals as 'Critical Editors' of Wikipedia." Opening with a consideration of Wikipedia's bias, this chapter first details the many ways that Wikipedia's content and editorship are skewed in favor of white male editors from the Global North. I also explore how Wikipedia's neutrality mandate and its ban on "original research" have helped exacerbate these biases. To counter these problems, I outline an approach that I call "critical editing." Predicated on four key features—power awareness, critical literacy, desocialization, and self-organization/self-education—the critical editor is a person who can scrutinize articles for unconscious bias, thereby making the site more accurate and just. The chapter ends with an open-ended list of ways that a critical editor can read and edit Wikipedia, pushing back against the looming danger of oft-invisible biases in the process.

Following a brief conclusion, this book closes with a glossary of keywords that readers can consult whenever they come across a new term or unfamiliar Wiki-slang.

I WANT YOU TO BECOME A WIKIPEDIA EDITOR

Comprising millions of articles that cover almost every category imaginable, Wikipedia is the most-visited general reference encyclopedia currently available, with its daily users including everyone from schoolchildren to medical professionals. But despite this overwhelming popularity, most people who use the site for general research have never edited it in any meaningful way. When I ask people why they haven't tried their hand at editing, most respond with a rather straightforward answer: "I don't know how." As such, this book has been my attempt to ameliorate some of this unfamiliarity.

Armed with knowledge about Wikipedia's history, the way it works, and its weaknesses, my hope is that readers of this book will log onto the site, create their own accounts, and start editing articles about their interests in a productive and critical way. This means that if you—like me—are an amateur autodidact who believes in the power and potential of the encyclopedic format, consider this book to be a call: I want you to become a Wikipedia editor! It does not matter if your contributions are big or small; simply by logging on and pitching in with your expertise, you are helping enrich and maintain one of the world's greatest informational resources.

A NOTE ON CONVENTIONS

Before jumping into my fuller consideration of Wikipedia, I would like to briefly explain a few typographic and stylistic choices that I have employed in the book.

- First, if you see a word or phrase that is <u>underlined</u>, that means that a Wikipedia article with that exact name exists. I will be using this underlining method to quickly cite pertinent articles.
- Second, **bold** words refer to buttons or links that a Wikipedia editor can press when navigating the site (e.g., **Edit source** refers to the edit button found at the top of an article).
- Third, "display text" (i.e., text that you would see when you visit a Wikipedia article) is rendered in Helvetica font, like this. This mimics the way the text actually appears on the site.
- Fourth, lines of wikitext, code, or search queries have been shaded and rendered in Courier New font `like this`. This was done to emulate the syntax highlighting text editors commonly use when displaying code.

It is also worth noting that this book is focused primarily on the English version of Wikipedia. As such, any mention of "Wikipedia"—except where otherwise noted—refers to the specific site located at https://en.wikipedia.org/. (Having said that, because other language editions of Wikipedia use the same software as the English site, much of the content in this book can be applied to non-English Wikipedias, too.)

With all of that clarified, let us begin.

1

The History of Wikipedia

Whenever you type a query into one of the many search engines out there, it seems as if one of the first links almost always is to a Wikipedia article. It does not matter if the topic of your search is obscure or well known, Wikipedia is there, offering information that is just a hyperlink away. For individuals who grew up online, the omnipresence of Wikipedia often goes unquestioned, as if its existence were simply a fact of the internet. This assumption, however, skips right over Wikipedia's very real origin story.

In this chapter, my goal is to center this story by taking a stroll through history, exploring the cultural context in which Wikipedia emerged. First, I will discuss many of the famous encyclopedists of yesteryear, situating Wikipedia firmly in a tradition that dates back millennia. I will then recount the story of the ill-fated "Nupedia" project—an encyclopedic project coordinated at the turn of the twenty-first century by internet entrepreneur Jimmy Wales and philosopher of knowledge Larry Sanger. After reviewing the problems that doomed Nupedia, I will turn our attention to Wikipedia itself by chronicling its birth and early years. I then explore the debate about Wikipedia's accuracy and reliability, demonstrating in the process that hyperbolic fear and skepticism of the site is fundamentally misplaced. I close the chapter with a snapshot of Wikipedia at the start of 2022, briefly outlining its relative size, its editor count, and how it compares to other encyclopedias in terms of size.

A BRIEF HISTORY OF ENCYCLOPEDIAS

From the cuneiform tablets of Sumer to the Library of Alexandria, humans have been aggregating extant knowledge for thousands of years. But when it comes to the explicit practice of synthesizing what has already been written for later reference, perhaps it is best to start with the masters of informational reappropriation: the Romans.[1] As a people, the inhabitants of the Eternal City were fascinated with the knowledge of other cultures (especially the Greeks), and consequently many Roman writers endeavored to compile this knowledge into books that other Romans could read. Among the more prominent of these informational bricoleurs were Cato the Elder (author of *Praecepta ad filium*, a collection of maxims), Varro (author of the *Disciplinae*, a compendium of the liberal arts), Celsus (author of *De Medicina*, a compilation of medical knowledge based on older Grecian sources), and Cicero (whose numerous speeches, treatises, and letters thoroughly survey a bevy of topics, including religion, philosophy, rhetoric, and the Roman legal tradition).[2] But of all the Roman writers, the one who comes the closest to what we would now call an "encyclopedist" is Pliny the Elder.

A Roman naturalist and military leader who lived in the first century AD, Pliny the Elder was a learned man and collector of information who spent almost every available moment having a slave read to him. After accumulating a collection of "20,000 noteworthy facts . . . from one hundred authors,"[3] Pliny decided to compile everything into one massive compendium: the *Naturalis Historia* (in English, the *Natural History*). This work is exhaustive in its scope, covering everything from the philosophical (e.g., the nature of reality) to the practical (e.g., how to sow beans). One major innovation of Pliny's was the introduction of a handy index at the beginning of his work, which allowed readers to find the exact "article" (for lack of a better term) they were interested in reading. In the work's preface, Pliny explains that such an index was included because the *Naturalis Historia* was not meant to be read "cover to cover"; instead, Pliny clarifies, a reader should use the index to find key information when the need arises.[4] *Naturalis Historia* truly was a reference work.

Needless to say, the *Naturalis Historia* was a groundbreaking development, and it would go on to be a popular reference work for hundreds of years after Pliny's death. (Regarding its impact, Robert Collison notes that in the Middle Ages, "no self-respecting [European] library was without a copy" of the *Naturalis Historia*).[5] In time, however, Pliny's work was eclipsed by another work of informational synthesis: Isidore of Seville's twenty-book compendium, the *Etymologiae* ("The Etymologies"), published in AD 625. In this work—which was inspired by and explicitly cites the *Naturalis Historia*—Isidore attempted to detail the whole of knowledge via the (often wildly wrong) etymological history of key words.[6] Due to the breadth and scope of its coverage, Isidore's work was copiously copied by medieval scribes (almost one thousand handwritten manuscripts dating from the Middle Ages are extant), and it was cited by myriad scholars and would-be etymologists up to the invention of the printing press in the fifteenth century.[7]

So far in this brief history, I have focused exclusively on Europe, but such an obsession ignores the rich encyclopedic traditions of other, non-European cultures. During the Islamic Golden Age, for instance, myriad writers such as Ibn al-Nadim (fl. AD 960), Ibn al-Nafis (fl. AD 1250), and Al-Nuwayri (fl. AD 1300) compiled encyclopedias that cataloged the religious, scientific, and philosophical ideas flowing throughout the Islamic world at the time.[8] One of the most impressive of these works was the *Rasā'il Ikhwān al-Safā'* (commonly referred to as the *Epistles of the Brethren of Purity*), which distilled a diverse range of scholarly information into fifty-two essays. Compiled by the titular "Brethren of Purity" for the purpose of attaining salvation via knowledge, the *Rasâ'il* is a massive collection of information that has been hailed as "one of the great works of Arabic literature."[9]

The ancient Chinese, too, were masters of writing informational compendia. In AD 220, for instance, Emperor Cao Pi (r. AD 220–226) of the Wei state ordered his scribes to create a work that summarized the totality of knowledge so that he might be a more efficient ruler. The finished work, called the *Huang lan*, comprised eight million characters across forty sections. Unfortunately, by the time of the Song dynasty (AD 960–1279), this massive work had been lost.[10] Centuries after Cao Pi's encyclopedia was compiled, the Yongle Emperor (r. AD 1402–1424) of the Ming dynasty commissioned a similar project: the *Yongle dadian*. This work, published in 1408, was truly gargantuan; written by a team of about two thousand scholars over a period of four years, it featured a total of 370 million characters spread out across eleven thousand volumes. Alas, by the dawning of the twentieth century, most volumes of the *Yongle dadian* had also been lost—the victims of theft, fire, or mismanagement. Today, only several hundred volumes remain.[11]

Around the time that the *Yongle dadian* was being studiously assembled, Europe was undergoing something of an encyclopedic revolution, sparked largely by Renaissance humanism and the creation of the printing press. It was in this milieu that humanists coined the word "enkuklopaideia" by mistakenly compounding the ancient Greek phrase, *enkuklios paideia*.[12] Although the original phrase meant something like a "well-rounded education," for the Renaissance humanists, the new compound came to mean a work summarizing the "circle of knowledge."[13] In time, many works of pedagogy and philosophy began to feature the word "encyclopedia" in their title, but the historian Ann Blair argues that the first work to both use the word in its title and resemble what we would now recognize as a proper reference work was Johann Heinrich Alsted's *Encyclopaedia septem tomis distincta*, published in 1630.[14] This work, which comprised seven volumes, represented Alsted's arduous attempt to produce a *methodica comprehensio rerum omnium* (that is, a "methodical schematization of all things").[15]

The encyclopedic fervor of the Renaissance picked up pace during the Age of Enlightenment (ca. the seventeenth and eighteenth centuries), and within this crucible of rationality the concept of the "modern encyclopedia" was fully forged. Arguably the first of these revolutionary compendia was the *Encyclopédie* (released 1751–1772), written in French and edited by Denis Diderot and Jean d'Alembert. At the time, this work was highly scandalous because it advocated the supremacy of reason over anything else—including the

Catholic Church.[16] Later, in 1768, Colin Macfarquhar, Andrew Bell, and William Smellie published in English the *Encyclopaedia Britannica*, which further shook up things by alphabetically listing specific terms (e.g., "star," "light") alongside longer treatises on general subjects (e.g., "astronomy"), "with plentiful cross references from the one type of entry to the other."[17] Both *Encyclopédie* and the *Encyclopaedia Britannica* were revolutionary because they not only collected knowledge, but also democratized that knowledge so that people other than just the extremely wealthy could have access to it.

In the twentieth century, when modernist thought was at its zenith, encyclopedic concepts even more ambitious than those of the past were being dreamed up, of which perhaps the most famous is H. G. Wells's "Permanent World Encyclopaedia." The disaster that was World War I had led Wells to fear that humans had become too ignorant, and he believed that the only cure for this ignorance was for everyday people to have access to information usually reserved for only "a cultivated minority" of scholars.[18] In a 1937 letter to *Harper's Magazine*, Wells thus proposed an idea for a massive encyclopedia—what he idiomatically referred to as a "world brain"—that would function as a "synthesis of bibliography and documentation with the indexed archives of the world."[19] Great writers the world over, Wells wrote, could be employed to write and translate articles, thereby ensuring that the "whole [of] human memory can be . . . made accessible to every individual."[20] Unfortunately, the world ignored Wells's proposal, and two years after the publication of Wells's letter, humanity had lapsed into another destructive world war.

In the decades following WWII, the popularity of encyclopedias boomed, and in the United States especially, it became a mark of middle-class success for your family to have its own encyclopedia set. Many publishers seized on this belief by sending salespersons door-to-door to sell sets. During this era, the leading encyclopedia was arguably *Encyclopaedia Britannica*, although other reference sets—such as the *World Book* and *Collier's Encyclopedia*—also managed to find success.

By the end of the twentieth century, many publishers embraced the potential of computer technology by digitizing encyclopedias and offering them for sale via CD-ROMs or through the internet. (Perhaps the best example of these "digital encyclopedias" was Microsoft's *Encarta*.) The digitalization of encyclopedias helped solve the encyclopedic issue of access, but another problem with the encyclopedia format had to be solved: encyclopedias go out of date very quickly. How might publishers use digital technology to overcome this issue? In 1997, computer scientists Eric M. Hammer and Edward N. Zalta[21] published an article titled "A Solution to the Problem of Updating Encyclopedias" that attempted to answer this question. In the work, the two proposed

> a "dynamic" encyclopedia that is published on the Internet. Unlike static encyclopedias (i.e., encyclopedias that will become fixed in print or on CD-ROM),

the dynamic encyclopedia allows entries to be improved and refined, thereby becoming responsive to new research and advances in the field. Though there are Internet encyclopedias which are being updated on a regular basis, typically none of these projects [give] the authors direct access to the material being published. . . . [The] dynamic encyclopedia [on the other hand] gives the authors direct access to their entries and the means to update them whenever it is needed [all] without sacrificing the quality of the entries.[22]

Hammer and Zalta were not the first people to suggest the need for an online encyclopedia—in 1993, for instance, the internet enthusiast Rick Gates proposed a freely accessible online repository of knowledge dubbed "Interpedia."[23] But Hammer and Zalta's article was ingenious for its suggestion that an encyclopedia's many authors should be given the ability to directly update their own articles whenever necessary, thereby decentralizing the content production. Although this idea never really caught on with mainstream encyclopedias, it would eventually become an integral part of the Wikipedia project that emerged only a few short years after the publication of Hammer and Zalta's article.

NUPEDIA: THE FLAWED PROGENITOR

Wikipedia, of course, did not pop into existence fully formed and ready for use. Instead, the site was the serendipitous result of a years-long endeavor to create a free, online encyclopedia called Nupedia, which never quite got off the ground. And as Wikipedia cofounder Larry Sanger has argued, "The origin of Wikipedia cannot be explained except in" the context of Nupedia.[24]

But before I take a look at this project, perhaps it is best to start with the individual who is largely responsible for both Nupedia and Wikipedia: Jimmy "Jimbo" Wales. Jimmy Wales was born in 1966 in Huntsville, Alabama, to a family that cared deeply about education. Wales was an insatiable reader in his childhood, and he spent many hours poring over copies of the *Encyclopedia Britannica* and odd copies of the *World Book* that he could find (a kindred spirit); these experiences would lead to his lifelong love of the encyclopedic format. When he was only sixteen years old, Wales began attending Auburn University, graduating in 1986 with a bachelor's degree in finance. He was then accepted to the University of Alabama's PhD program in finance but left in 1988 with a master's degree.[25] Wales subsequently attended Indiana University to earn a PhD in finance, but after finishing his doctoral course work, he "got bored" and left the program in 1994 to work as a finance trader in Chicago.[26]

During his college years, Wales was introduced to the wonders of the then-fledgling internet, and soon he devoted copious amounts of time playing around in various multiuser dungeons ("MUDs" for short), where he and a bevy of virtual compatriots would engage in elaborate fantasy quests.[27] According to the *Encyclopedia of Alabama*, these MUDs "contributed to his later views on non-hierarchical . . . Internet entities," such as Wikipedia.[28] The internet also allowed Wales to dabble in one of his other passions: philosophical discussion. Wales had long been a fan of Ayn Rand's Objectivism, a rational egoist line of thought that stresses the importance of individualism, capitalism, and logic. In 1989, he consequently set up an e-mail listserv called the "Ayn Rand Philosophy Discussion List," through which he and other like-minded individuals would trade messages about epistemology and the like. One of those who joined in on the debates was Larry Sanger, a student of philosophy at Reed College and the Ohio State University. Sanger had little patience for Objectivists "because they pretend to be independent-minded and yet they follow in lockstep behind Ayn Rand," but he and Wales nevertheless became friends due to their shared interest in asking the big questions about life.[29]

In 1998, Wales relocated to San Diego and cofounded the internet portal Bomis, a proto-search engine that became infamous for helping people find porn and other adult resources. But for Wales, a site like this was only a stepping-stone on the path to achieving his dream: to use Bomis's capital to fund the creation of a massive encyclopedia, which would be hosted for free online. This aspiration, almost certainly sparked when he was a kid reading old *Britannica* copies, was furthered by his interest in Rand's philosophy. (One of Objectivism's key concepts is that the external world is real and can be accurately measured by humans; this logically implies that the whole of reality—given enough time, effort, and precision—could be documented and described by human researchers.)[30] Wales also assumed (rightfully) that emerging digital technology would soon enable large-scale encyclopedic writing the likes of which history had never seen before, and with enough people onboard, a truly gargantuan compendium of knowledge could be assembled.

In January 2000, Wales and Sanger reconnected via e-mail, whereupon the former offered the latter a job at Bomis, helping Wales create his dream encyclopedia. Wales was drawn to Sanger—who at the time was finishing a doctorate in philosophy at the Ohio State University—because he wanted a "philosopher" to helm the project. (In fact, so set was Wales on this that he made it a term of Sanger's employment that he finish his PhD as soon as he could.)[31]

Needless to say, Sanger accepted the job—after all, not every day is a freshly minted philosopher of knowledge offered a funded job helping to create a giant encyclopedia—and the two got to work. Wales served as the project manager and the "idea guy," and via Bomis, he also provided the capital needed to get the project moving.[32] Sanger, on the other hand, was tasked with figuring out the logistics of the project. "I spent the first month or so thinking very broadly about different possibilities," Sanger wrote in a book chapter about the origin of the site. "I [also] wrote quite a bit . . . and discussed quite a bit with both Jimmy and one of the other Bomis partners, Tim Shell."[33] From these conversations, a clearer vision of their project began to emerge, and in time, they dubbed their nascent site Nupedia.

Wales wanted the finished product to be freely accessible by all, and so he created the "Nupedia Open Content License," which allowed readers to copy and repost Nupedia articles free of charge, as long as they attributed the work to Nupedia (later, in 2001, the site would adopt the more widely used GNU Free Documentation License).[34] Wales was also adamant that the encyclopedia should be "volunteer-built," meaning that, in principle, anyone could participate if their work was of quality. Although not opposed to the idea in general, Sanger was a bit leery about letting just anyone write for the project. For one thing, he felt that "something really could not be a credible encyclopedia without oversight by experts."[35] Sanger thus began to reach out to some of his contacts in the world of academia, sharing with them his ideas for the site. Many of those interested in contributing were also invited to become members of the site's advisory board, a sort of governing presidium that helped shape the project's policies.[36]

Another concern that Sanger had was with the problem of subjective editor bias; thus, he insisted that the site adopt a policy of neutrality to ensure that "articles [would] not represent any one point of view on controversial subjects, but instead fairly represent all sides."[37] To further guarantee the quality of articles and ameliorate the problem of authorial bias, Nupedia's review board also instituted the following seven-step article approval process:[38]

1. **Assignment:** The review board assigns an article to a writer, who is to be an "expert" in her field.
2. **Find a lead reviewer:** Separately, the review board locates an expert to peer-review the finalized article draft.
3. **Lead review:** The reviewer conducts a blind read of the article and either rejects it due to critical issues, or proposes suggestions to improve it. The author of the article implements suggestions as needed.
4. **Open review:** Once the article is judged to be of quality, other site reviewers as well as members of the public are invited to comment on the article and propose suggestions.
5. **Lead copyediting:** The article is copyedited by two dedicated copyeditors.
6. **Open copyediting:** The article is copyedited by the public.
7. **Final approval and markup:** The final version of the article is marked up in XML and then freely published online.

At the time, this review process was fairly innovative, balancing a respect for expert knowledge with the principles of open contribution; in many ways, it presaged the more collaborative review processes that contemporary publications such as *Hybrid Pedagogy* use.[39] Unfortunately, the review process proved to be far too slow: Nupedia went live in March 2000, and by the end of the year, only nine articles had been published.[40] By the end of 2001, the number had risen to only twenty-five.[41] If this project were to survive, it needed some serious tinkering.

ECCE, WIKIPEDIA! THE BIRTH OF THE ENCYCLOPEDIA ANYONE CAN EDIT

When it became clear that the article production pipeline was stalling Nupedia's growth, Sanger and Wales retreated to the drawing board, spending the winter of 2000–2001 thinking of innovative ways to overcome the site's problems. Luckily, inspiration would strike on January 2, 2001, when Sanger met up with Ben Kovitz, a friend he had gotten to know through e-mail-mediated philosophy discussions. Sanger expressed his frustrations with how slowly the Nupedia project was developing, which led Kovitz to suggest that the Nupedia team employ a wiki to speed up article production.[42]

At this point in the chapter, it is perhaps worth taking a tangent to discuss the nature of a "wiki." After all, when discussing Wikipedia with folks who have never really used it before—and yes, these people do exist—one of their first questions is usually a variation of, "What exactly does *Wiki* mean?" The unique term, derived from the Hawaiian term "wikiwiki" (which means "quickly"), can be briefly glossed as a website that allows users to modify its contents. Although the wiki format is commonly associated with "Web 2.0" (a somewhat nebulous term referring to social and user-created Web content, such as Wikipedia), the concept was actually introduced in 1994 by Ward Cunningham, a Portland, Oregon–based computer programmer who at the time oversaw a website called WikiWikiWeb. Cunningham wanted his site to grow into an information repository for other programmers; to speed up this development, he opened it up for editing, allowing any visitor to add to or change information on the site.[43] In today's ever-changing world of digital media, this might seem somewhat banal, but at the time of its introduction, the wiki was positively revolutionary, proving that websites did not need to be static, nor did content production need to be closed off.[44] (And why, might one ask, did Cunningham choose a Hawaiian word as the name for his site? It is all because of a ride Cunningham once took on the "Wiki Wiki Shuttle" when visiting the Honolulu International Airport. It is a catchy term, after all.)[45]

The wiki is, by its very nature, a malleable type of site, so it is hard to provide a one-size-fits-all definition for the concept. Nevertheless, Ward Cunningham and Bo Leuf, in their book *The Wiki Way*, argue that the wiki concept is based around three core ideals:

- First, a would-be contributor does not need to download additional software or undergo any specialized training to edit a wiki; the only things a contributor needs are a Web browser and an internet connection.

- Second, wikis encourage "topic associations" through the use of in-text hyperlinks. These links allow a reader to jump from one topic to another with ease.
- Third, wikis are collaborative spaces that seek to enmesh readers in the "ongoing process of creation." Put another way, the wiki platform, by the very nature of its design, encourages readers to become contributors, too.[46]

Today, many types of software can support a wiki's infrastructure, but arguably the most popular is MediaWiki. Written in PHP to serve the needs of the Wikimedia project, MediaWiki was developed by programmers Magnus Manske and Lee Daniel Crocker in 2002. It currently serves as the main "engine" supporting Wikipedia, and it supports a variety of non-Wikipedia related wikis such as RationalWiki (a wiki dedicated to skepticism),[47] Ballotpedia (a site dedicated to American politics),[48] and Fandom Inc. (a Web service that hosts wikis related to various fandoms and media franchises).[49]

With all this in mind, let us jump back to 2001. When Sanger learned of the wiki model, he was immediately curious, believing it had the potential to solve some of Nupedia's problems. Sanger soon hatched an idea: What if a wiki were set up alongside Nupedia? On this wiki, anyone—not just the "experts"—could contribute content, and if the review board deemed the content to be of quality, it could then be moved to the main Nupedia site. Basically, Sanger saw the wiki as a useful tool to generate rough drafts written by the masses.[50] Sanger shared his idea with Wales, and although the latter was skeptical at first, he agreed to Sanger's proposal. On January 10, 2001, Sanger sent an e-mail to the Nupedia mailing list announcing an accompanying Nupedia wiki, which he lauded as "the *ultimate* 'open' and simple format for developing content."[51]

Although some initial comments were positive (Nupedia's chief copyeditor Ruth Ifcher responded: "I like the idea. We need some place that is less structured to toss around ideas and interact"),[52] other members of Nupedia's review board were less than thrilled by this development. The historian Michael Kulikowski, for instance, shot off an e-mail that read, "I think we're going to make utter jackasses of ourselves. . . . Gimmicks are no good substitute for the academic seriousness with which this whole project began."[53] Likewise, the classicist Carl Anderson responded, "The question seems to me . . . whether we want to invest our time in silliness."[54]

As a result of this pessimism, Sanger and Wales decided that if the wiki experiment were to go forward, it would need to be clearly differentiated from the "serious" project that was Nupedia. So Sanger suggested that they call the new site "Wikipedia"—a "silly name for what was at first a very silly project."[55] Bomis subsequently purchased the "Wikipedia.com" domain name, and the website went live on January 15, 2001; just like that, Wikipedia was born.[56]

The first article created for the site was a page called HomePage. Created by the official Bomis account, User:Office.bomis.com, the initial version of the article was brief and to the point: "This is the new WikiPedia!"[57] (During this time, User:Office.bomis.com also created articles for WikiPedia, PhilosophyAndLogic, and UnitedStates.)[58] On January 17, Larry Sanger announced via the Nupedia mailing list that Wikipedia was ready to go, and in no time, a respectable number of users were visiting the site and contributing to its contents. Wikipedia—in stark contrast to Nupedia—began to grow at an explosive rate: by the time February 2001 rolled around, 173 articles had been created, and by the end of the year, the article count stood at a staggering 16,967 entries.[59] Much of this growth can be chalked up to increasing press coverage: On July 25, 2001, a post about Wikipedia was shared to the popular technology site Slashdot, which sent hundreds of curious readers to the burgeoning Web resource. On September 24, 2001, a second Slashdot post brought an even larger wave of new editors.[60]

The Slashdot swells of 2001 proved that people were fascinated with the idea of a free encyclopedia that anyone could edit, but the influx of amateur encyclopedists also brought with it its own problems. "In the project's first nine months or so," Sanger explained, "I recall saying casually . . . that experts and specialists should be given some particular respect when writing in their areas of expertise."[61]

Such an opinion, however, did not sit well with many of the site's editors, who by and large believed that Wikipedia's radically democratic ethos precluded privileging traditional experts. These users began to clash with Sanger, the self-described "symbol of opposition to anarchism," leading to colorful online arguments. Unfortunately, Sanger found himself outgunned, so to speak; his role as Wikipedia cofounder was one with little executive authority, meaning that all he could really do was trade sharply worded messages with a growing group of editors. In 2002, Bomis—which had tried and failed to fund Wikipedia via Web advertisements—laid off Sanger to save money,[62] and in 2003, Sanger officially severed ties with the project due to philosophical differences about the importance of expert knowledge. Although he had played a major role in the encyclopedia's founding, Sanger would go on to become one of Wikipedia's biggest critics.

But despite losing one of its cofounders, Wikipedia continued to grow. On June 20, 2003, Wales founded the Wikimedia Foundation, a charitable 501(c)(3) intended to foster the Wikipedia brand and ensure that it would remain a noncommercial endeavor. Soon thereafter, a variety of Wikimedia-backed websites were established that followed in the free and open spirit of Wikipedia, including Wikibooks (July 10, 2003), WikiQuote (July 10, 2003), Wikisource (November 24, 2003), and the Wikimedia Commons (September 7, 2004).[63]

In 2005, Wikipedia hit another milestone when it surpassed Dictionary.com as the most-popular general reference source online.[64] Much of this popularity can be attributed to its visibility in search engine results. (In 2005, for instance, the Wikipedia *Signpost* noted that "the Google web crawler went from having 3 million Wikipedia pages indexed in March to more than 25 million in July.")[65] Wikipedia was like the proverbial snowball rolling down the hill: it just kept growing and growing. By the end of 2010, Wikipedia editors had created an astonishing 3.5 million articles.[66]

WIKI-PANIC! THE ACCURACY AND RELIABILITY CONTROVERSY

Wikipedia's rise in visibility, however, quickly engendered skepticism about its reliability. After all, if anyone—regardless of academic qualifications—can edit the site, how are readers to know what is or is not true? These criticisms began to mount. In 2005, the prominent journalist John Seigenthaler lambasted the site as a "flawed and irresponsible research tool" after his article was vandalized.[67] Likewise, in 2007, Michael Gorman, a prominent librarian who at the time was president of the American Library Association, decried the site for furthering the "flight from expertise."[68] For these authors, Wikipedia was nothing more than a flaming trashcan of drivel and libel. Of course, as will be discussed in chapters 5 and 6 of this book, it is perfectly reasonable to approach Wikipedia articles with skepticism, but for many seasoned Wikipedia editors (including myself), contemporary critiques of Wikipedia that echo Seigenthaler and Gorman's opinions are often hyperbolic, sensationalistic, and a bit outdated.

First, it is important to note that much of the worry about "reliability" was fomented when the site was relatively new. In the early days, the site was something like the Wild West, and it was common for articles to feature paragraphs of text with nary a citation; nowadays, information on Wikipedia that is not backed up with a reliable reference is often (but not always) culled by other editors. This is not to say that Wikipedia's content is now error free, but, rather, that the site's policies have evolved over the years, moving largely in a direction that privileges referencing and accuracy over raw content creation.

Another problem with the mistrust about Wikipedia's content is that time and time again, both academic and popular studies have determined that although the site contains errors, its content is roughly as reliable as other published reference works. Perhaps the most famous of these studies was the 2005 review published by the science journalist Jim Giles in *Nature*, which concluded that "high-profile [errors about science on Wikipedia] are the exception rather than the rule," and that the site is roughly as reliable as the *Encyclopaedia Britannica*.[69]

Subsequent studies have continued to support *Nature*'s findings: a 2007 study by the *Library Journal*, for instance, declared that the site's coverage of pop culture and current affairs is fairly accurate, and although its scientific articles do have their shortcomings, "good content [still] abounds."[70] Likewise, a 2011 article by the political scientist Adam R. Brown found that many articles are victims of recency bias or "errors of omission," but that the content itself is "often very good"—especially for "recent or prominent topics."[71] Similarly, a 2014 study by Jona Kräenbring and others published in *PLOS One* quantitatively concluded that the "accuracy of drug information in Wikipedia was 99.7%±0.2% when compared to the textbook data."[72] Again, these studies do not prove that Wikipedia is an error-free wonderland, but they do suggest that much of the worry about the site is due to an ignorance of reality. Wikipedia is far from perfect, but it is also far from the tar pit of misinformation that some take it to be.

WIKIPEDIA BY THE NUMBERS: STATS AND DEMOGRAPHICS

In the 2010s and 2020s, Wikipedia continued to grow. Today, it is both the biggest and most-used reference source online; as of December 2021, the site included more than 6.42 million articles, which have been collectively edited more than one billion times[73] by 42.77 million registered users (of whom around 120,433 are considered "active," meaning that they regularly edit the site).[74] In 2021, the site averaged 243.7 million pageviews a day,[75] and when all the language editions of Wikipedia are counted together, the site is the fourteenth-most-visited website worldwide, according to Alexa rankings; it is also the most-visited .org page.[76]

In terms of article count, Wikipedia is a behemoth that towers over its de facto rival, *Encyclopaedia Britannica*, whose 2010 print edition contained 40,000 articles, and whose online-only version contains 120,000 articles. In fact, so much bigger is Wikipedia that if someone were to print the site in book volumes of roughly the same size and paper weight as those used for the 2010 edition of the *Encyclopaedia Britannica*, it would take a staggering 3,013 volumes to account for the entirety of Wikipedia; hundreds of additional volumes would be necessary were you to also print an index of articles as well as a listing of every editor who helped write those articles. In comparison, the 2010 version of the *Encyclopaedia Britannica*—index and all—takes up only thirty-two volumes.[77]

Now that I have contextualized the complex history of Wikipedia and demonstrated its relative size, the following chapter will explore in greater detail the site's philosophy and its expectations of new editors.

2

The Wiki-Ethos

What to Know Before You Edit

Wikipedia is the digital home to thousands of editors, who over the years have developed a sophisticated and fascinating set of cultural norms and expectations. Unfortunately, for new editors otherwise unfamiliar with the intricacies of the Wikipedia community, these norms and expectations can be opaque, confusing, and sometimes contradictory on their face. As such, many new editors almost immediately face a flood of questions:

> What exactly is Wikipedia?
> How does the site really work?
> What type of content should editors contribute?
> What sort of behavior is allowed and what is not?

In this chapter, I intend to answer many of these questions by situating them in the overall philosophy of the site. The first half of this chapter is dedicated to a detailed look at Wikipedia's "five pillars": the quintet of principles that contextualize the site, outline its mission, and establish its content parameters. The chapter closes with an unofficial list of dos and don'ts that I have compiled over my many years as an editor. By the time readers reach the end of this chapter, they should have a sufficient understanding of Wikipedia's fundamental ethos and what is expected of them as an editor.

THE FIVE PILLARS OF WIKIPEDIA

In 2005, the user User:Neutrality recognized that many Wikipedia neophytes struggled with acclimating to the "Wiki-ethos" that guides the site. User:-Neutrality consequently wrote an essay titled Wikipedia:Five pillars, which summarizes in five points (the titular "pillars") the "fundamental principles of Wikipedia." These pillars—which are explicated in the following sections—are fairly straightforward,[1] and when taken together, I believe they nicely sum up the spirit of the site and the ideal modus operandi of its editors.

Wikipedia Is an Encyclopedia

The foundational pillar of Wikipedia is the idea that it is an encyclopedia. This might seem self-evident—after all, is the site not called Wiki*pedia*?—but it is an important point to emphasize, as it defines the site's purpose. By first and foremost situating itself in the encyclopedic tradition, Wikipedia makes clear that it is to function as a "compendium of knowledge" in the mold of ever-popular reference works such as the *Encyclopaedia Britannica*.[2]

To further explain what is meant by Wikipedia "being an encyclopedia," many editors have echoed the approach of negative theology by choosing to describe what the site is *not*. This is perhaps best illustrated in the essay Wikipedia:What Wikipedia is not, in which it is argued that, among other things, the site:

- **is *not* a dumping ground for random information**—Wikipedia was created as a space in which world knowledge could be broken down and summarized into coherent articles. Key elements in this process include the *summarization* and *organization* of knowledge. Summarization means that a Wikipedia article should not simply list every fact or feature about a given topic; information that is included needs to be notable and relevant. Likewise, organization means that articles should be divided into logical subsections, each focusing on a specific aspect of the topic in question.
- **is *not* a dictionary**—Although dictionaries and encyclopedias are both reference works, they serve different purposes. Broadly speaking, an encyclopedia comprises articles that summarize key information about *subjects* (such as persons, places, things, events, experiences, etc.) that are either specific (e.g., Aral Sea) or general (e.g., sea). A dictionary, on the other hand, lists all the words in a language, how those words can be used, what these words mean in brief, and what parts of speech they belong to. In other words, a dictionary is fundamentally a lexical reference work. Because Wikipedia focuses on more than just lexical information, it should not be thought of as a dictionary.[3]
- **is *not* a social networking site**—Working tirelessly behind every Wikipedia article is a network of editors whose interactions have given rise to a robust subculture. Although Wikipedia's policies actively foster this community, social interaction is secondary to the site's main purpose of creating a massive encyclopedia. Thus, editors should not view Wikipedia exclusively as a place to forge social relationships. This does not preclude

the development of friendship; it simply means that everything that an editor does on Wikipedia should, in some sense, be done in the name of furthering the site's goal.

- **is *not* a Web directory**—Many Wikipedia articles are categorized as "lists," meaning that they catalog articles related to one another. However, list articles and the entries they contain (like all articles on Wikipedia) need to be notable if they are to be included on the site. Thus, Wikipedia is not the place for extensive directories that indiscriminately list non-notable genealogical information, context-free quotes, telephone numbers, upcoming events, or commercial products.
- **is *not* a free advertising space**—Wikipedia was created to summarize knowledge about notable topics. It was not created as a place for people to promote themselves or advertise products. Promotional content of this sort is verboten because it is almost never written in an unbiased, objective way (thereby violating Wikipedia's neutrality requirement), and it often lacks reliable sourcing that establishes its notability. To avoid any hints of self-advertising, it is generally recommended that editors do not modify articles with which they have some close connection.
- **is *not* a place to publish your opinions or ideas**—All content in a Wikipedia article needs to be backed up with a published, reliable, and verifiable source. This means that neither an editor's unpublished ideas nor their personal opinions belong on the site. If you have a novel idea and you want the world to know about it, consider publishing your thoughts through a reliable and notable third-party venue such as a journal or book publisher. If your idea is eventually deemed notable, it will likely find its way onto Wikipedia.

Wikipedia's Content Is Neutral, Citational, and Never Original

The second pillar of Wikipedia concerns the site's content. To keep articles consistent and orderly, Wikipedia's rules stipulate that all articles must be written from a neutral point of view, they must cite reliable sources, and they must not contain original research. Let me consider each of these points on its own:

Wikipedia's Content Is Neutral

All content on Wikipedia must be written from a neutral point of view (commonly referred to as "NPOV"). This means that editors need to check their personal biases when working on articles, and they should refrain from adding content that heavily skews an article toward one viewpoint. Editors are also required to craft articles so that they accurately represent the larger scholarly conversation, proportionately covering all major views about a given topic. This does not mean that "all sides" must be equally represented in an article—one half of the Evolution article, for instance, does not need to focus on creationist rebuttals, nor does the Ancient aliens theory deserve repeated mention in the Ancient Egyptian technology article. This "equal time" approach would give undue weight to certain viewpoints, creating a "false balance."[4] Instead, proportionate coverage means that all major viewpoints should be discussed relative to their appearance in the existing literature. This means that if Theory A dominates much of the literature about Topic X, the Wikipedia article on Topic X should focus heavily on Theory A.

It is common for critics of Wikipedia to cite NPOV as one of its biggest flaws. For detractors, the big issue here is that Wikipedia defines neutral editing as reflecting what the extant body of human knowledge has to say. Unfortunately, hundreds of years of institutionalized racism, sexism, classism, and myriad other "-isms" have engendered a systemically biased "body of human knowledge" that inequitably privileges the ideas of white, straight men at the expense of pretty much every other category of person.[5]

For critics of Wikipedia, "neutral" editing can thus never really be neutral, because this approach simply reaffirms the supremacy of that systemically biased body of knowledge, which in turn allows systemic injustice to live on.[6] This critique of NPOV[7] is, to my mind, a solid point that cuts to the heart of what may be Wikipedia's greatest weakness. In chapter 6, I will consider this issue in greater detail, outlining several ways we can help clear the site of systemic bias.

Wikipedia's Content Is Citational

With a few exceptions, everything on Wikipedia needs to be backed up by a reliable source. Such a reference generally possesses three traits:

- First, reliable sources must be published. Usually, this means that a source has been subjected to review by a third party and then professionally released for public consumption. Self-published sources can be glossed as sources that are created without editorial oversight and are released by an individual without a traditional publisher. Examples of self-published sources include social media posts, websites, blogs, forums, and vanity press books. Because these sources are often the products of nonexperts and may be inaccurate, they are usually prohibited on Wikipedia. An exception to this proscription are self-published sources that were published by a notable individual, are not unduly self-serving, and are not being used to back up controversial or exceptional claims about third parties.[8]
- Second, a reliable source must have a reputable author and/or publisher. To determine this information, you might need to do some investigating (see chapter 6 for more on this). Ask yourself if a source's author is a well-respected expert in their field, or if the source's publisher is known to peer-review its publications. Another good idea is to see what the author or the

publisher has released in the past. When in doubt, reach out to the editors at the <u>Wikipedia:Reliable sources/Noticeboard</u> and see what they have to say.

- Third, a reliable source must be verifiable. This means that another editor could conceivably locate the source and confirm its contents. This does not mean that a source needs to be *easily* accessible—simply that it *is* accessible. For instance, although an out-of-print book might be difficult to track down, it can still be accessed given enough time, patience, and interlibrary loan requests; information from a non-recorded interview, however, cannot be accessed. If one cannot locate an information source, it cannot be used on Wikipedia as a source.

If the source you want to use checks all three of these boxes, you can likely add it to an article without any problems.

Wikipedia's Content Is Never Original

Finally, Wikipedia articles must not contain "original research" (commonly abbreviated as "OR"). As was discussed in the earlier section about Wikipedia's encyclopedic nature, original research refers to novel assertions, hypotheses, theories, or claimed breakthroughs that have not already been published in a reliable source, such as a journal or a book.[9] If I were to discover the secret to cold fusion, for instance, I could not create a Wikipedia article that details my findings because this would constitute original research. If I wanted my discovery to find a home on Wikipedia, I would first need to have my findings published by a reputable source, whereupon it could be added to the site.

Why does Wikipedia prohibit this sort of research? The simplest answer is that the ban serves as a quality-control mechanism, ensuring that claims on the site are limited to those that experts have vetted. Original research is also likely to contain opinions, the inclusion of which would be a clear violation of NPOV. The ban on original research can thus be seen as a reinforcement of the site's NPOV policy.

Wikipedia Is Free

Despite millions of visitors dropping by each day, Wikipedia has refused to charge subscription fees or run ads (turning down what likely would be billions of dollars in ad revenue),[10] all in the name of remaining a free-to-use, non-commercial endeavor.[11] In our age of widespread monetization and cutthroat hyper-capitalism, the fact that Wikipedia has not only remained free but also thrived is, frankly, remarkable. But Wikipedia's steadfast commitment to open knowledge has bred ignorance about the site's copyright status. Many people, for instance, assume that the text of Wikipedia is in the public domain. This is an understandable assumption, but it is incorrect.

In reality, when an editor contributes to an article and clicks the "Publish Changes" button, they agree to release their contributions under the "Creative Commons Attribution Share-Alike 3.0" license (often simply referred to as "CC BY-SA 3.0").[12] A "Creative Commons license" is a nifty legal agreement that enables a copyrighted work to be freely circulated as long as certain usage rules are followed. The particular CC BY-SA 3.0 variant that Wikipedia uses means that any content added to the site may be reused by anyone, for any purpose, even if it is for commercial gain. The catch is that those who reuse the site's content must attribute the material to Wikipedia and indicate if any changes were made; if someone does make changes to the material, they are required to release their new derivative work under the CC BY-SA 3.0 license, too.

For the sake of demonstration, let us pretend that you want to take some text from the <u>Little brown bat</u> article and incorporate it into a book you are writing. What would the ideal attribution statement look like in this case? First, the statement should clearly identify the Wikipedia article and its author(s); this can be done by simply providing the article's URL (listing the editors who contributed to the article is unnecessary, given that the URL links to the article's History page, which functions as an author list).[13] Second, the attribution statement needs to indicate whether any changes were made. This can be done with a phrase such as "This work is a derivative of . . ." or "This work interpolates text from . . ."[14] Finally, the attribution statement should include information about which Creative Commons license the work has been released under. So, in our example, the result would look something like this:

> This work is a derivative of the Wikipedia article "Little brown bat" (https://en.wikipedia.org/w/index.php?title=Little_brown_bat&oldid=1039245408), and it has been released under the CC BY-SA 3.0 license (https://creative commons.org/licenses/by-sa/3.0/).

But Wikipedia-cribber, beware! Just because *most* of the text on Wikipedia has been released through a free license does not mean that *all* of the text is up for grabs. Quotations, excerpts from published works, and song lyrics, for instance, almost always retain their original copyright; because of this, these short snippets of text can only be added into articles if they satisfy the criteria for "fair use." (In American copyright law, "fair use" refers to the lawful reuse of an otherwise copyrighted work for purposes of criticism, commentary, or discussion.) If, for the purposes of another project, you want to reuse copyrighted material that is also being used on Wikipedia under a claim of "fair use," you will need to seek permission from the copyright holder(s), not Wikipedia.

Wikipedians Should Act Civilly

When it comes to dealing with other editors, "civility" is the name of the game, and everyone—from anonymous IP users to veteran admins—is expected to treat fellow contributors with respect. One key element of civility is to assume good faith. This means that when an editor (or a group thereof) does something that seems problematic or unproductive—for example, someone adds poorly formatted text in an article, or deletes part of an article for no clear reason—other editors should approach the situation under the assumption that the person "causing trouble" might simply be confused, misguided, or inexperienced.

The best thing to do in a situation like this is to message the "problem editor" via their talk page and explain your thoughts. Tell them in plain, uncharged language why you think their contributions might not be ideal, and provide them with the chance to explain themselves. At no time should an editor make personal attacks.[15] Many times, assuming good faith and striking up a conversation neutralizes a brewing conflict. Other times, however, the conversation will confirm that the editor is trying to be disruptive or engaging in wanton vandalism. In these cases, it is best to undo any damage and then report the editor in question at the Wikipedia:Administrator intervention against vandalism portal.

Despite "civility" being a key component of the Wiki-ethos, Wikipedia unfortunately has developed a reputation as being something of a hostile work environment. A 2010 study of 1,238 former editors who had since left Wikipedia, for instance, found that 12 percent of those surveyed left because the "atmosphere [was] unpleasant," and 24 percent left because "some editors made Wikipedia difficult"[16] (the problem is especially acute for female editors, as I will discuss in chapter 6).[17]

Part of the issue likely is due to the semi-anonymity given to editors, as studies have shown that online anonymity increases the likelihood that people will act in hostile ways.[18] Another issue is that editors can zealously guard articles that they have worked on tirelessly; if a newer editor comes along and changes something that a more experienced editor has created, the more experienced editors often lash out to protect their article from harm. Of course, some editors are just rude. In the second part of this chapter, I will discuss some tips and strategies to help overcome rudeness and general incivility on Wikipedia.

Wikipedia Has No Firm Rules

At first, the assertion that Wikipedia has no firm rules sounds anarchic, as if the site is the digital equivalent of the Wild West. Such a statement also seems to vindicate Alan Kirby's critique of Wikipedia as "Michael Foucault's final fantasy: the release of knowledge from its incarceration in power structures, its liberation from systems of dominance, oppression, exclusion."[19] If there are no firm rules—a wiki-skeptic might ask—does that mean there are no clear-cut ways to "correctly" edit? Does it mean that anything goes? If this is all true, Wikipedia can at best be seen as a postmodern mishmash of nonsense and fluff. I hear this critique time and time again, but it fundamentally misunderstands the "no firm rules" pillar.

The idea that there are "no rules" does not mean that editors are free to do whatever they want. Instead, it is a pithy way of saying that Wikipedia is fundamentally built on what Robert Cummings and Matthew Barton call an "ethos of continual modification and improvement."[20] This means that editors implicitly understand that the site's policies (of which there are many) are far from immutable. If enough editors push for a change to a specific policy, then that policy very well might change. Similarly, if people widely support a specific policy, and some other editor continually violates the policy, that editor likely will be sanctioned.

It might be easier to think of Wikipedia's system of governance as a more informal version of something like the U.S. Constitution: in the United States, the text of the Constitution is law—that is, until that text is amended. Technically, you could argue that the Constitution, like Wikipedia, has no firm rules, given that legal ways exist through which the document can be overhauled.

Having said that, I will concede that Wikipedia's rules are *not* as rigidly enforced as those in a federal constitution. In fact, among Wikipedia editors, there is a long-standing tradition is that "if a rule prevents you from improving or maintaining Wikipedia, ignore it."[21] Again, on the surface, this might seem anarchic; in actuality, it is just a provocative way of saying, "Use your common sense and do whatever you think will make Wikipedia better." If an editor violates an established guideline or policy with good intentions, in the spirit of improving the site, it might ruffle some feathers, but chances are, any fallout will be minimal. Conversely, if an editor who has actively vandalized hundreds of pages tries to cite the "ignore the rules" maxim, they likely will be blocked; after all, as the Wikipedia essay Wikipedia:IARMEANS notes, "While ignoring all rules is all right, it is subtly but importantly different from deliberately breaking them."

Wikipedia's malleable system of rules and policies ultimately is founded on consensus making.[22] This is not the same as simply voting; after all, Wikipedia is not a democracy.[23] Instead, consensus making is a process that makes "an effort to incorporate all editors' legitimate concerns while respecting Wikipedia's policies and guidelines."[24] As many scholars have already noted, the way in which Wikipedia editors come to a consensus mirrors the Quaker-based consensus model, pioneered by the Religious Society of Friends.[25] Similarities between the two methods of consensus making include the following:

- Participants are encouraged to "deeply"[26] and "actively"[27] listen to one another—even if they do not agree with what others are saying.[28]
- All participants should be allowed to voice their opinions.[29]
- The discussion should be overseen by a moderator[30] who "steers but does not dominate."[31]
- Participants should respond to, rebut, or build off comments made by others in a constructive way that avoids personal attacks.[32]

- The process of consensus building should, to the degree possible, synthesize all participants' points.[33]

Much like Quakers, Wikipedia editors aim for "unity, not unanimity";[34] this means that not every single editor has to completely agree with consensus, but all should respect whatever decision the group ultimately makes.[35]

THE DOS AND DON'TS OF BEING AN EDITOR

Now that I have explored the five pillars that support the overall Wiki-ethos, I believe it useful to cover some dos and don'ts of being an editor. But before I begin, I want to emphasize that the suggestions covered in this section are just that—suggestions. They are not codified laws, nor are they rigid guidelines that must always be adhered to. Instead, they are general rules of thumb that I have developed based on my personal experiences with Wikipedia.

Do Your Homework

It might go without saying, but whenever you edit a Wikipedia article, it is best if you know a bit about the topic in question.[36] This does not mean that you must be an expert to work on the site; it simply means that before you make considerable changes to an article, you should do your homework: carefully research the topic that you are interested in. Take a deep dive into the literature. Document what you learn. Jot down and scrutinize your sources. Reach out to other editors and turn it into a group project. But most importantly, take your time—Wikipedia does not have a deadline, so you have no reason to rush your work.[37] If you focus less on how fast you can write an article and more on the quality of your research, the contributions that you make to Wikipedia likely will be informed and of quality.

I learned all this the hard way back in 2013 when I was editing the article on Pedra da Gávea, a mountain in Brazil. At the time, I was in a class about fringe science and "fantastical archaeology." As I was doing course readings, I stumbled across the aforementioned Wikipedia article, which featured a section about the pseudo-archaeological "theory" that Pedra da Gávea was engraved with an inscription by ancient Phoenicians. I was fascinated with how this bogus narrative had evolved, so I spent a few days working on the mountain's article. Initially, I thought I had done a pretty good job researching the topic: I had invested time in tracking down dusty old books that mentioned the inscription, and I expanded whole sections about what people thought it meant. I even borrowed through interlibrary loan an old book written in Portuguese that had a beautiful painting of the supposed inscription. All of this work led me to think I had whipped up a solid article, so I submitted it for "good article" consideration.

Unfortunately, in my zeal to improve the article, I had concentrated almost entirely on the pseudo-archaeological claims about the mountain and not the mountain itself. During the "good article" review, an editor brought up this issue, so I hastily dropped in some geology information that I had found during a quick search on Google Books. My work here was sloppy. Because I did not do due diligence, I badly misinterpreted one source, injecting a burst of misinformation into the article. Fellow Wikipedian User:AfadsBad quickly noticed my edits and published a WordPress post about my supposed incompetence. I was humiliated. Although AfadsBad's belligerent tone was, in my opinion, rather uncalled for (see the following section), the problems that they raised with the article were valid. The fiasco taught me a lesson: before substantially editing a Wikipedia article, be sure that you know what you are talking about. Otherwise, you likely will embarrass yourself.

As an aside, when working on articles about living individuals,[38] it is imperative that you go above and beyond when doing your homework, as these articles are heavily scrutinized to prevent the addition of contentious or potentially libelous content. (The last thing you want to do is be sloppy, misinterpret a source, and land Wikipedia in a lawsuit.)

Don't Get into Fights

> I will always assume good faith on the part of my fellow editors and will be civil at all times, even to those who are not civil to me. I will not attack my fellow editors or disrupt Wikipedia to make a point. If involved in a content dispute, I will not engage in edit warring and will instead discuss contested edits and/ or seek dispute resolution. —The creed of User:Vicenarian, which succinctly covers how best to handle conflict

Wikipedia is a collaborative environment in which dozens of editors are forced to "share their toys" (so to speak), and because of this, the site often bears witness to editor disputes. Many of these are but minor quarrels that quickly fizzle out, whereas others are bona fide wiki-brawls. The most common type of wiki-brawl is an edit war, in which two (or more) contributors spitefully undo one another's contributions. Edit wars usually follow a trademark back-and-forth pattern: An editor will modify an article, and then an opposing editor will swoop in and undo that change. The first editor, incensed, will then revert that second editor's revision. The second editor then returns the favor, and the spectacle repeats ad nauseum. Edit warring is a disruptive behavior that can very easily spiral out of control, and as such, it is a banned practice; to enforce this prohibition, the site has instituted a "three-revert rule" (Wikipedia:3RR), which maintains that "an editor must not perform more than three reverts on a single page—whether involving the same or different material—within a 24-hour period."[39] If an editor violates this policy, they run the risk of being blocked from editing for a period of time, and if they become a habitual "edit warrior," they might earn a ban.

Fights can also break out when editors are simply rude or belligerent to one another. Here's a hypothetical example: Let's say that you spent the past few hours working on an article about a topic with which you have long been fascinated. You take a break for a bit. When you return to the site, you discover that another editor—let's call him "Ed Hominem"—has reverted your contributions. To add insult to injury, Ed called your contributions "unproductive" in his edit summary (which, for those new to Wikipedia, is a short text box where contributors describe how their edit changes a page). The nerve! What should you do? Many a person's first instinct is to fight: you might want to revert Ed's contributions and kick off an edit war. Or maybe you think of a really juicy insult. Although all of these options may promise satisfaction in the moment, they are all less-than-ideal ways to handle the situation.

Instead, refrain from letting your emotions go wild. True, Ed's comments were mean, but you will not improve Wikipedia by firing off an insult (no matter how witty). Next, assume that Ed was acting in good faith. Look at your contributions. Did something about your edits anger Ed? Did you misinterpret a source, or add material that Wikipedia's guidelines prohibit? Is it possible that Ed misread one of your contributions, mistaking it for vandalism? If these explanations do not readily explain Ed's behavior, initiate a conversation. Reach out to Ed's user talk page, or the talk page of the article that you both are editing. Create a new section and politely ask Ed if he could explain why he not only reverted but also denigrated your contributions. (It never hurts to throw in a little bit of humor here to lighten the mood, but be careful, as humor can easily be misinterpreted as mocking.) An invitation to talk often is enough to diffuse a situation, but if a more spirited debate breaks out, stay civil and focus on refuting what you believe to be the error in Ed's reasoning.

Usually, after enough back-and-forth debate, both sides will begin to see where the other is coming from, and the situation will begin to resolve itself. But what if in this case Ed is a real ne'er-do-well, and he answers your call to parley with a chorus of insults. (*O tempora, o mores!*) At this point, consider just walking away; despite what many people think, you do *not* have to win every argument on the internet, and some people are just not worth the effort. But if you really feel the need to fight the fight, so to speak, reach out to another editor and ask him to unofficially negotiate the conflict. (One way to do this is to post a request on the Wikipedia:Third opinion page.)

If nothing else works, and the situation spirals into blatant editorial misconduct, the last option is to bring it to Wikipedia:Arbitration/Requests to begin the arbitration process—a process overseen by a dedicated "arbitration committee" that considers the situation and "impose[s] binding solutions to Wikipedia conduct disputes that neither community discussion nor administrators have successfully resolved."[40] Arbitration is something like Wikipedia's court of final appeal, so just as you don't contest a parking ticket before the U.S. Supreme Court, don't take a simple spat to the arbitration committee.

Do Disclose Conflicts of Interests

Editing with a "conflict of interest" refers to the modification of articles that pertain in some way to you, your family, your friends, your place of employment, and so on. Basically, if an article exists to which you have a personal connection, you have a conflict of interest (from here on, abbreviated as "COI"). It can sometimes be tricky to determine if one has a conflict of interest; as Wikipedia notes, "How close the relationship needs to be before it becomes a concern on Wikipedia is governed by common sense."[41] A simple rule of thumb is that if you know the person "in real life," you likely have a COI. For instance, if your father is a renowned poet, or your best friend is a rock musician, you would have a COI if you edited articles about them. If, however, you are simply writing about your favorite poet or a musician with whom you do not have a close personal relationship, you likely do not have a COI.

Editors with a COI are not in and of themselves barred from Wikipedia, but they must be mindful of their position, contributing in ways that are neither duplicitous nor unduly self-serving. As always, the name of the game is good faith, and if an editor with a COI contributes in such a way, they are unlikely to get into trouble. Editors have several ways to avoid accusations that they are inappropriately editing with a COI.

First, simply be transparent about your situation; this is arguably the "easiest way to gain the community's trust, get help, and avoid embarrassing revelations of misconduct."[42] Editors can disclose this sort of information by posting to the Wikipedia:Conflict of interest/Noticeboard, mentioning any COIs on their user page, creating a discussion section on an article talk page, or making note of COIs in an edit summary. Another way to head off criticism about a COI is to "keep your distance" from articles with which you might have a close connection. If you feel that a change is needed to an article related to you, start a discussion. Reach out to other editors, explain who you are, and then put forth any ideas you might have about improving the articles in question.

On a related note: If you hope to get a job writing articles for people or companies in exchange for money, be warned. Wikipedians do not think highly of this behavior, as many believe that money throws any semblance of neutrality out the window. Being a paid editor—even if you disclose your conflicts of interest—is seen as a parasitic act, and it will often earn you a reputation as a pariah. On top of this, if you do *not* disclose your conflict of interest, you run the risk of covert advertising, which is often illegal. I believe it is best to avoid paid editing all together, given all the baggage associated with it.[43] Note that Wikipedia's articulation of "paid editing" usually exempts the work of editors who, under the auspices of a cultural institution (e.g., a museum, a library, a historical society), share their institution's resources or expert knowledge simply to make the site a better resource.

Don't Plagiarize or Violate Copyright

According to Wikipedia, "Plagiarism is taking credit for someone else's writing as your own, including their language and ideas, without providing adequate credit."[44] Many people plagiarize not out of malice but, instead, out of ignorance.[45] In an attempt to ameliorate this issue and dispel any confusion about Wikipedia's citation practices, the Wikipedia article Wikipedia:Plagiarism has broken down the site's policies into three simple rules of thumb:

1. **Incite**—Always include an inline, footnoted citation when adding content to an article.
2. **In-text**—When paraphrasing, best practice is to add an in-text attribution that clearly states from where you are pulling your information.
3. **Integrity**—Ensure that your contributions cite their source(s) in a clear way.

The three words are simple enough on their own, but what do they mean in practice? To answer this question, let me demonstrate with one of my beloved hypotheticals. Pretend that I have in front of me a book titled *Animals of Ooo*, written by the explorer Phlannel Boxingday, and on page 56, I see this sentence: "Near Lake Szelezon, there lives a most curious little beastie, the 'fluff-fluff,' and it is easily one of Ooo's most delightful creatures."[46] Now pretend that I am editing the Wikipedia article about the fluff-fluff, and in doing so, I add the following content to the page:

> Near Lake Szelezon, there lives a most curious little beastie, the "fluff-fluff," and it is easily one of Ooo's most delightful creatures.

This addition would constitute plagiarism. Not only have I directly copied material from a source, but I have also omitted a citation or an attribution note. Now, say that I recognized my error and changed the sentence to read:

> Near Lake Szelezon, there lives a most curious little beastie, the "fluff-fluff," and it is easily one of Ooo's most delightful creatures.[1]
> [1.] ^ Boxingday, Phlannel. *Animals of Ooo*. p. 56.

This is certainly better; I now have a clear citation, but I still have a problem: I have copied, word for word, the source text into the article. Whenever you copy text directly from a source, always put quotation marks around the words that you reuse; it is also a good idea to explicitly attribute the source within the text itself with signal phrases:

According to the explorer Phlannel Boxingday, "Near Lake Szelezon, there lives a most curious little beastie, the "fluff-fluff," and it is easily one of Ooo's most delightful creatures."[1]

[1.] ^ Boxingday, Phlannel. *Animals of Ooo*. p. 56.

This sentence does not plagiarize, because I have cited my source and quoted appropriately. But Wikipedia's guidelines recommend that I take this all a step farther by *paraphrasing* some of my source, rather than quoting it all:

The fluff-fluff was described in Phlannel Boxingday's book *Animals of Ooo* as "curious" and "one of Ooo's most delightful creatures."[1]

[1.] ^ Boxingday, Phlannel. *Animals of Ooo*. p. 56.

Thankfully, on Wikipedia, accidental plagiarism is not the death sentence it often is in academia. If you ever are accused of plagiarism on the site, recognize what went wrong, try your best to clean up the issues, and—most important—learn from the experience.

At this point it is worth noting that plagiarism is *not* the same thing as copyright infringement: the former is a violation of ethics, whereas the latter is a legal issue. (If I try to pass off Lewis Carroll's *Through the Looking-Glass* as my own work, I am definitely plagiarizing, but I am *not* committing copyright infringement, because Carroll's work is in the public domain. Conversely, if I quote, cite, and then reproduce the entirety of the *Harry Potter* series, I'm not plagiarizing because I'm giving credit, but I *am* violating copyright.) That said, copyright also comes into play on Wikipedia; after all, when you edit an article, you agree to license your copyrighted material (i.e., your textual contributions) via a CC BY-SA 3.0 license so that others can use it. This means that you can only add material to the site that you hold the copyright to; copying and pasting text from the newest edition of *Encyclopaedia Britannica* into a Wikipedia article, for instance, would be unacceptable because you do not own that work. In fact, if you were to add that text to Wikipedia, you would be violating copyright laws. As such, if you do not know the copyright status of a text that you want to edit into Wikipedia, hold off on editing it in. It is better to be safe than to violate copyright.

Do Work with Others

Although some editors prefer to work on articles by themselves, the fact of the matter is that Wikipedia is a massive collaboration. Being able to work with others is a key skill that all editors should possess. Having said that, some editors (including, at times, yours truly) can have a hard time editing with others—this is especially true when one editor's vision for an article clashes spectacularly with the edits of other Wikipedians. (I can say from experience that investing hours of your life into writing an article, only for someone else to change things in an instant, can be incredibly frustrating.) But in times like these, it is important to remember that Wikipedia's policies state that, regardless of the labor an editor has put into an article, "No one . . . has the right to act as though they are the owner of a particular article . . . nor [do they have] any right to dictate what the article may or may not say."[47] Because Wikipedia is a collaboration, its articles are effectively owned by everyone. Wikipedia is the ultimate commune.

Although an editor cannot own an article, it is customary for Wikipedians to steward articles into which they have invested time and energy.[48] (I myself steward hundreds of articles, most of which I have promoted to "good" or "featured article" status. Because it was so much work to clean up and promote these articles, I keep my eye on them, reverting unnecessary vandalism and the like.) Article stewardship is all about protecting the accuracy and presentation of an article; this means that if an editor swoops in and productively overhauls an article, that article's steward should have no problem with the changes. Unfortunately, the real world is rarely ideal, and magnanimous stewardship can very easily devolve into a snappy and aggressive sort of possessiveness. If you run across an editor you think is overly domineering about select articles, always assume good faith and open a conversation either on their talk page or the talk page of the article.

Don't Vandalize

Vandalism in the context of Wikipedia refers to any editing that attempts to disrupt the site and stymie the spread of knowledge. For years, Wikipedia has been haunted by the specter of vandalism (how many teachers told you not to use the site because "anyone can edit it to say anything they want"?), but thankfully, many instances of vandalism are easy to fix. This is because most vandals are content to simply delete all the text on a page or add swear words into articles—acts that do not go unnoticed for very long. Vandalism usually is committed by anonymous editors (a 2007 vandalism study conducted by Wikipedia's Counter-Vandalism Unit, for instance, concluded that 97 percent of vandalism can be traced to anonymous IPs),[49] but some vandals do create accounts. Regardless, any vandals—registered or not—run the risk of being blocked, sometimes indefinitely, if they horse around.

As I alluded to earlier, belief is widespread that Wikipedia is a heavily vandalized hellscape. The truth is that the site has several safeguards that prevent vandalism from being anything worse than a time-consuming nuisance. For one thing, many of the most-visited (and thus, most likely to be vandalized) pages are locked down with editing restrictions, which prevent unregistered editors from changing article content. Other articles are regularly patrolled by senior editors, who use a tool called a watchlist to detect whether malicious changes have been made. (I, for instance, use my watchlist to keep an eye on the Adventure Time and The X-Files articles.) Wikipedia is also swarming with helpful bots that monitor edits for suspicious activity. One of the most active of these, ClueBot NG, uses machine learning to revert hundreds of bad edits every day.[50]

If you want to make Wikipedia a better, more comprehensive source, it goes without saying that you should refrain from vandalizing articles. Not only is it a malicious act that disrupts an otherwise noble project, but it is also an easy way to get blocked.

Do Have Fun

I strongly believe that contributing to Wikipedia should be an enjoyable experience—after all, what other site lets you write articles on topics about which you care deeply in a way that also helps create and maintain the world's biggest free encyclopedia? But even though the site is a paradise for many, it is not uncommon for editors to experience bouts of wiki-stress. Maybe a talk page debate spirals out of control, or an article into which you invested significant time and energy has been repeatedly vandalized. Whatever the cause, if you feel like your cortisol levels shoot up every time you log in to make an edit, it might be time for you to take a break from editing. Leave Wikipedia for a bit and return when you feel energized and happy to be back. This will prevent burnout and allow you to reconnect with the joy inherent in editing articles.

3

Getting Started

Making Your First Edits

So far, I have situated Wikipedia in the encyclopedic tradition and explicated the philosophy that supports the site, but I have yet to talk about how one actually edits the site. For those chomping at the bit, the wait is finally over—in this chapter I tackle the question head-on, detailing the oft-mysterious practices by which Wikipedians modify the site's content.

For those unfamiliar with how the site's pages are arranged, I kick things off with a look at the "anatomy" of your average Wikipedia article. I then explore the ways that anonymous and registered editors differ from one another, and I show you how to set up an account. After this, I introduce you to the "Visual Editor," a powerful tool that enables editors to format text, generate wikilinks, place citations, and insert section headings without having to know the complexities of wikitext (complexities that will be explored in greater detail in chapter 4). Although there is more to editing Wikipedia than what is covered in this part of the book, you should nevertheless find this chapter to be a succinct introduction to the essential tools and methods that will allow you to become a master editor.

THE ANATOMY OF A WIKIPEDIA ARTICLE

The layout of the average Wikipedia page may appear, at first glance, to be rather simple, but when you take a closer look, you will see that there is more to an article than meets the eye. For readers unfamiliar with the specific structure and elements of a Wikipedia page, I recommend that you first familiarize yourself with the basics of an article's "anatomy" by consulting figure 3.1 and table 3.1.

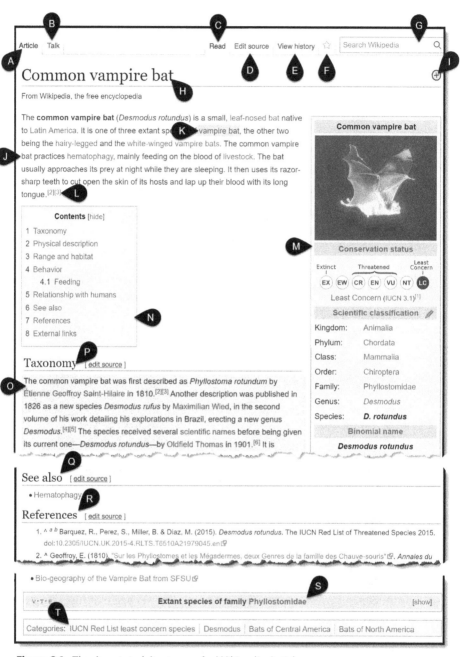

Figure 3.1. The Annotated Anatomy of a Wikipedia Article

Table 3.1. Elements of a Wikipedia Article

Label	Feature	Description
A, B	"Article" and "Talk" tabs	When you visit a Wikipedia article, the "Article" tab is selected by default, presenting you with encyclopedic content. Clicking on the "Talk" tab, on the other hand, will take you to an article's talk page, which is a "behind-the-scenes" space where editors can discuss the main article.
C	"Read" tab	Similar to the "Article" tab, the "Read" tab is automatically selected when you visit an article. This ensures that you see the final, formatted page.
D	"Edit" tab	Clicking this tab will open up the article for editing. (If the Visual Editor is active, the tab will simply read "Edit"; if you are working with the wikitext editor, however, this tab will read "Edit source.")
E	"View history" tab	Clicking this tab will redirect a reader to the History page, which lists all the edits made to a given article, along with information about who made them and when they were made.
F	"Add to Watchlist" tab	Clicking this tab will either add the article to or remove it from your Watchlist.
G	Search box	The Wikipedia Search box can be used to search the site. To locate an article, type its name in the bar and hit enter. If an article title matches your query, you will be brought to that page. If a match is not found, Wikipedia will instead list articles that might be related to your query.
H	Article title	An article's title will appear below the row of tabs in a large script. On Wikipedia, article titles are written using sentence case style, which means that only the first word and any proper nouns[1] are capitalized (e.g., <u>Sentence case</u>, rather than <u>all lowercase</u>, <u>Title Case</u>, or <u>CamelCase</u>). No two articles are allowed to have the same title. To differentiate between articles with the same main name, disambiguation information enclosed in parentheses is added to an article's title. If two or more topics share a name, but one is arguably more popular than the other(s), only the lesser-known topic(s) will receive parenthetical disambiguation. This is why biographical information about the famous author Henry James is located at <u>Henry James</u>, whereas information about the lesser-known Welsh theologian of the same name is found at <u>Henry James (Dean of Bangor)</u>.

(continued)

Table 3.1. (*continued*)

Label	Feature	Description
I	Article quality/ status icons	In its upper right-hand corner, an article might contain one of several small symbols; these can tell you about the quality or status of the article. A small green circle with a cross in the middle (⊕) means that the article has officially earned "good" status. Likewise, if you see a gold star (★), you know that the article is one of the site's few "featured" articles. "Good" and "featured" articles have been vetted by other editors, making them among the site's best pages. Conversely, if you see a padlock icon (🔒), that means that a page is locked. Often, this indicates that the page is a favorite target for vandals.
J	Article lead	Articles begin with a short introductory section, usually referred to by editors as a "lead" (and sometimes a "lede"). This section functions as the article's abstract, hitting all the key points that are explicated in greater detail within the body of the article itself. Because this section summarizes information that is cited later on, a lead does not need to be as rigorously cited as an article's body.
K	Article wikilinks	"Wikilinks" are hyperlinks that take a reader to other Wikipedia articles. Wikilinks that lead to existing pages appear as blue hyperlinks; wikilinks to pages that do not yet exist will appear as red hyperlinks. Policy recommends that terms should only be wikilinked once per article, upon their first mention.
L	Inline citations	Inline citations on Wikipedia take the form of superscript Arabic numerals enclosed in brackets. These markers follow immediately after most forms of punctuation, with no space separating the punctuation from the marker, like this.[1] The numeric value of the footnotes is determined by the order in which they are cited in an article.
M	Infobox	An infobox is a panel that summarizes important features about an article's subject. Infoboxes usually are located in the right-hand corner of an article (to the right of the lead section, but below the title), and they often contain links to related articles. It is also common—but not required—for an infobox to feature an image of the article's subject matter.

Label	Feature	Description
N	Table of contents	If an article contains more than three section headings, Wikipedia will automatically generate a table of contents listing all the headings in the article. (This table will appear immediately before the article's first heading.) The table of contents is hyperlinked, and clicking a heading will take the reader to that section of the article.
O	Article body	The body of an article comprises all the text following the article's lead and table of contents. Unlike the lead, which provides a general overview of a topic, an article's body text is more detailed in its coverage, and the content must be backed up by reliable sources.
P	Section headings	Longer articles are almost always divided into distinct sections, each with its own topical focus and unique heading. This division allows for a greater, more microscopic level of coverage than what might otherwise be possible. Although most articles use only one or two heading levels, some articles feature as many as five. (Note that next to each header title is an **Edit source** link. Clicking this will open the wikitext editor, allowing you to edit that particular section.)
Q	"Further reading," "See also," and "External links" sections	At the bottom of an article, they are often sections labeled "Further reading," "See also," and/or "External links." A "Further reading" section contains citations relevant to an article but not directly cited. A "See also" section similarly lists pertinent Wikipedia articles that have not already been linked to in the main text. Finally, an "External links" section lists off-site resources of interest. (An article should contain only a few external links, and these links must contain information that is "accurate and on topic."[2])
R	References	References appear near the bottom of an article and are listed in the order they are cited in the text; if you click on the caret mark (^) next to a reference's number, you will be taken to the place in the article where this reference is cited. If a single reference is cited multiple times, hyperlinked letters will follow the caret, e.g., 1. ^ a b c d Citation Text. Clicking on these small letters will take the reader to each place that this one reference is cited.

(continued)

Table 3.1. (*continued*)

Label	Feature	Description
		Most citations include all or most of the fields required to source a claim (e.g., author, title, publisher, date). If, however, an article cites a single resource (e.g., a book) multiple times throughout, it is common for citations to be abbreviated. These shortened citations usually link to a "Bibliography" section containing a complete citational entry.
S	Navigation Boxes	Many articles feature navigation boxes. These are specialized templates that wikilink to related articles. This makes it easier for a reader to find articles on a similar topic. Navigation boxes usually are "collapsed," meaning that, by default, only a title is displayed; to reveal the contents of a navigation box, a reader must click on the **show** link.
T	Categories	Categories are used to sort articles into different, topically similar groups. Categories can, like an article's text, be added and removed by editors.

1. Including multi-word proper nouns, such as "University of Chicago" or "*The Count of Monte Cristo.*" When dealing with multi-word proper nouns, prepositional markers (e.g., "of"), noninitial conjunctions (e.g., "and") or noninitial articles (e.g., "the") are written in lowercase.
2. Wikipedia:External links.

CREATING AN ACCOUNT

When I walk people through Wikipedia for the first time, I am often asked whether I think it is better to edit anonymously or to create an account. It is a good question—and one that does not have a single "right" answer. If you decide to contribute as an anonymous IP editor, you will be able to access and edit almost every article or talk page on the site, excepting articles that have been locked (these pages, in the past likely popular targets for vandals, can only be edited by established editors). IP editors are also unable to create new articles or upload images; if they edit an article to include an external link, they will have to pass a CAPTCHA test before their change is accepted. Why are the abilities of IP editors so heavily limited? The simple answer is quality control: two decades worth of data show that anonymous editors are more likely than registered users to vandalize articles and abuse policy.[1] By restricting what IP editors can do, Wikipedia is nipping the problem in the bud. (Having said all that, many anonymous IP editors are productive, and IP restrictions are the unfortunate result of a few bad apples spoiling the barrel.)

If you choose to create an account, on the other hand, you will receive certain privileges that anonymous editors do not have, such as the ability to create articles and upload images. Creating an account on Wikipedia is fairly straightforward. To do so:

1. Navigate to https://en.wikipedia.org/wiki/Main_Page.
2. In the upper right-hand corner of the screen, click the **Create account** link.
3. This will redirect you to a new page, where you will be asked to choose a username and a password.
4. When creating an account, you can also enter your e-mail if you think you will need to reset your account one day. (This step is optional.)
5. Finally, pass a CAPTCHA security check and click **Create your account**. Just like that, you are ready to edit.

When picking a username, make sure not to choose a name that violates any of the rules listed at Wikipedia:Username policy. Do not choose a name that is offensive, overly controversial, promotional, or intentionally confusing. It is also advisable that you do not use your real name, or a username that makes you easily identifiable. If, at a later date, you decide to change your username, you will need to make a request at the Wikipedia:Changing username portal. Be aware that this is not a surefire process, and many name change petitions are rejected.

Only one person can use a username/account; this means that if a group of friends want to edit an article together, each of them will need to register their own account. Sharing one username—even if the contributions made through that account are productive—is strictly forbidden and can lead to that username being blocked. On the flip side, a single user should never (with a few exceptions)[2] create multiple accounts to edit articles. Using—and especially abusing—multiple accounts is referred to as "sockpuppetry," and it, too, can lead to editors being banned from the site.[3]

Common Types of Editors

Although all editors are equal in the eyes of site policy (see Wikipedia:Equality), not everyone is granted the same technical permissions or "rights." Some editors, for instance, can delete pages, whereas others can only edit them. An editor's abilities are ultimately determined by that editor's access level—something normally determined by how long an editor has had an account and how many edits they have made. Editors with the same access level are said to belong to the same "user group," the most common of which are outlined in table 3.2.

Despite what many people believe, Wikipedia admins are not the "leaders" of the site, nor do they wield their awesome godlike powers for personal gain. Adminship, instead, is—at least in theory—more about site maintenance and

Table 3.2. Common Types of Editors

User Group	Requirements	Privileges and Restrictions
Unregistered	None	Unregistered users can edit most articles, but they cannot create new pages or move existing ones. They also cannot edit certain pages that are protected. Unregistered users must pass a CAPTCHA test every time they add an external link to an article.
Registered	Requires a user to create an account	Registered users can customize their account preferences and keep track of their edits. However, until they fulfill the requirements necessary to gain autoconfirmed status, registered users face many of the same restrictions as unregistered users.
Autoconfirmed	An account must be at a minimum four days old and have also made ten edits to the site	Autoconfirmed users can create articles, move pages, and edit some protected pages. Autoconfirmed users do not have to pass a CAPTCHA test when adding an external link to an article.
Extended Confirmed	An account must be at least thirty days old and have made at least five hundred edits	These editors can modify pages that are under extended confirmed protection.
Administrator	Appointed following successful Request for Adminship (RfA) process	Administrators (usually referred to simply as "admins") are effectively the field marshal custodians of Wikipedia. These users can block/unblock registered users and anonymous IP addresses, adjust page protections, and delete or undelete articles. Their job is to help keep the site functional and running.
Bureaucrat	Appointed following successful Requests for Bureaucratship (RfB) process	Bureaucrats are a select group of users who can grant or remove admin privileges to other users. Bureaucrats are often (but not necessarily) admins.

behind-the-scenes upkeep. It is ultimately a custodial job; for this reason, those who become admins often are jokingly told they have been "given the mop."[4] Having said all that, it is undeniable that admins have a certain degree of clout, meaning that although they might not technically be in charge of the site, their opinions unofficially carry great weight.

NAVIGATING THE USER OPTIONS TOOLBAR

Once you have created an account, you are immediately given access to several tools that make editing, collaboration, and article upkeep easier. These tools are located in the **User options** panel, which is found in the upper right-hand side of the screen. Once you have logged into your account, your panel will look something like this:

👤 Lil Myotis 🔔 ▢ Talk Sandbox Preferences Beta Watchlist Contributions Log out

Your User Page

On the far left of the user options panel is a link to your own **user page**. This basically functions as an "About the Editor" portal where you are allowed to share a bit about yourself. Many editors choose to do this by listing the topic areas they are interested in or by showcasing articles that they are proud to have worked on. Other editors communicate additional information about themselves through userboxes. These are small, usually brightly colored boxes that visually and textually convey some aspect of an editor's identity. (One of my userboxes, for instance, identifies me as a member of the "Bats Wiki-Project," whereas another mentions that I am an intermediate reader of Latin.) The intricacies of userboxes are beyond the scope of this book, but if you want to learn more, visit the Wikipedia article Wikipedia:Userboxes.

If you have just created your account, the hyperlink to your **user page** will appear in red font, meaning that the page has not been set up. To create your user page, simply:

1. Click on the redlink. This will redirect you to a new page that reads: "Wikipedia does not have a user page with this exact name."
2. Underneath this statement, another link will read: **Start the User:Name page**. Click this link. (If a "Welcome to Wikipedia" box pops up, select the option that says **Start editing**.)
3. This will open the site's plain text editor, allowing you to create your user page. Because we have not covered the finer details of editing yet, go to the large white text box that takes up most of the page and write something simple such as `This is User:Name's user page` (replacing *Name* with your username, of course).

4. When you are ready to publish the page, scroll to the bottom of the edit window and click the button that says **Publish changes**.

The "Talk Page" Feature

Another feature that editors (both registered and anonymous) can access is a personal talk page, which can be visited by clicking the link in the user options toolbar that reads **Talk**. This page is effectively a portal where other editors can communicate with you. When another editor leaves you a message on your talk page—an act often colloquially referred to as a "pinging"—the **Alerts** (♠) and **Notices** (▭) buttons in the user options toolbar will notify you by visually indicating the number of unread messages you have (e.g., you might see something like ♠ or ▭).

To locate another editor's talk page, go to the search bar in the upper right of the screen and type User talk: followed immediately (without space) by the username of the editor you are trying to find, like this: User talk:Name. (For an example, if I wanted to send a message to my fellow editor, Big_Eptesicus, I would type User talk:Big_Eptesicus in the search bar.)

To leave a message for another editor, first go to their user talk page. At the top of the page, just under the user options toolbar, you should see a tab that says **New Section**. Clicking on this will open the site's wikitext editor (which will be the focus of chapter 4, so stay tuned). Next:

1. In the editor screen, you should see a **Subject** box. In the space provided, type a title for your message; think of this box like the subject line in an e-mail message.
2. Next, place your cursor in the big white box that takes up most of the screen and begin typing your message.
3. After composing your message, sign it by typing two minus signs followed immediately by four tildes: --~~~~. (These symbols will be converted by Wikipedia into your digital signature once the page is saved.)
4. When you are ready to post the message, scroll to the bottom of the edit window and click **Publish changes**.

After hitting this button, your message will appear at the very bottom of the other editor's talk page. It is worth noting that some editors choose to respond to messages on their own talk page, whereas others will reply on the talk page of the editor who contacted them. If you are expecting a reply, it is best to monitor both your own and the other editor's talk pages, just to be safe. (To learn how to respond to talk page comments, see the section in chapter 4 titled "Editing an Article's Talk Page.")

Your Watchlist

Now, let's go back to the user options toolbar and click the link that says **Watchlist**. This is a handy tool that allows you to "tag" select articles and keep a close eye on them; if someone makes a change to those articles, your Watchlist page will log the edit(s) for you to review. Your Watchlist will be an especially useful tool if you are working on articles that are heavily vandalized, or those that you have a personal stake in and want to maintain. To add an article to your Watchlist:

1. Search for the article that you want to keep an eye on.
2. When the article loads, go to the upper right-hand corner of the screen and click the tab emblazoned with a **Star** (★).
3. The star will briefly spin before changing from white to a shade of blue; this visually confirms that the article has been added to your Watchlist. (If you ever need to remove the page from your Watchlist, return to the article and click the star tab again. The star will briefly spin before reverting from blue to white.)
4. A pop-up window will inform you that the article has been added to your Watchlist.

Clicking the **Watchlist** link on your user options toolbar will take you to a page listing the articles that have been edited recently. (If you want to see *all* the articles on your Watchlist, click the **Watchlist** link and then click **Edit your list of watched pages**. Alternatively, you can type `Special:EditWatchlist` into the search bar.)

To better illustrate how the Watchlist feature works, let me provide an example. Let's pretend that I have added the Little brown bat article to my Watchlist. If another user were to edit this article, my Watchlist page would automatically update, displaying something like this:

September 21, 2021
```
◦ m 16:08 Little brown bat (diff  | hist) .. (+7) ..
  Big_Eptesicus (talk | contribs) (Small tweak to prose)
```

Thanks to this Watchlist notice, we know that User:Big_Eptesicus made a minor edit to the article on September 21, 2021, at 16:08 UTC. We also know that the user added seven characters to the article and included an edit summary, telling us they were copyediting the article. If I wanted to see exactly what User:Big_Eptesicus changed, I could click **diff**, and if I wanted to send the user a message, I could click the **talk** link to go to their talk page.

(As a personal aside, whenever I log onto Wikipedia, my Watchlist is the first page I visit. I use the diff option to review any edits made to articles that I am monitoring; if any of these edits are unproductive, I simply undo the changes. Conversely, if an editor adds content that improves an article, I like to reach out and thank them for their contribution.)

Your Sandbox

Next to **Talk** on your user options toolbar is also a link to your **Sandbox**.[5] A Sandbox is a page for experimenting with text and wiki-markup, making it the perfect place to practice your editing skills. Because these pages are not considered main articles, you have relatively free rein over their contents. (That said, your sandbox cannot contain copyrighted material or text that is uncivil.) Although other editors can access your sandbox, an unspoken rule prohibits editing other users' sandboxes without their permission. Seasoned users tend to use their sandboxes less as a place for experimentation and more as a storage space for article rough drafts or topics that they want to work on in the future. Whenever you test one of Wikipedia's editing features, it is advisable to do so in your personal sandbox; when you feel you are comfortable with the mechanics of editing, you can start editing the main site.

Your Contributions Page

The last user options tool that I want to talk about here is your **Contributions** page, which you can access by clicking the link at the top of the page, situated between "Watchlist" and "Log out." Clicking this link will take you to a chronological record of all the edits you have made as a registered editor. Each contribution log will look something like this:

- `16:08, January 18, 2017 .. (diff | hist) .. m (+7) ..`
  `Little brown bat (Small tweak to prose)`

Let's break down what this means: The first part of this entry logs the date and time[6] of an edit. The **diff** button will show you a before-and-after comparison of the article you edited, allowing you to see exactly what you changed. The **hist** button will redirect you to the history page of the article in question (we will discuss history pages later). The parenthetical number (in the example above, +7) denotes how many characters were added or removed in a particular edit; additions are proceeded by a plus mark (+) and displayed in green text, whereas removals are preceded by a minus sign (−) and are displayed in red. If an edit record includes an **m**, that means that the edit was tagged as a minor one. Edit records conclude with a simple link to the article you edited, along with an italicized copy of your edit summary (if you left one).

Near the bottom of the page, you will see a line that reads:

`(newest | oldest) View (newer 50 | older 50) (20 | 50 | 100 | 250 | 500)`

These links enable you to navigate your past contributions. Clicking **newest** will flip to your most recent edits, whereas clicking **oldest** will take you to your very first edits. You can also specify if you want to have your edits displayed in batches of 20, 50, 100, 250, or 500.

At the very bottom of the page is a **User info** box. **Articles created**, as the name suggests, will bring up a page listing of all the articles that you have created. The **Edit count** link, on the other hand, will redirect you to a Wikimedia Cloud Services page listing information about how many total edits you have made to the site.

THE BASICS OF EDITING WITH THE VISUAL EDITOR

Now that you have your account set up and you have explored your user options toolbar, it is time to start tinkering with Wikipedia's editing capabilities. For people brand-new to Wikipedia, it is advisable to start with the **Visual Editor** (sometimes abbreviated as **VE**). In the dark ages (i.e., a couple years ago), when people wanted to edit Wikipedia, they had to know the "ancient" art of "wikitext markup." For people not intimately familiar with coding, this markup was often frustrating to learn, and it is likely that many enthusiastic volunteers abandoned the site because they found editing too confusing. To make editing easier and more streamlined, the Wikimedia Foundation developed the Visual Editor, which is grounded on the idea that, when editing the site, "what you see is what you get" (commonly abbreviate as WYSIWYG). This guiding principle means that instead of redirecting you to a wikitext editor screen when you want to tweak an article, the Visual Editor lets you edit the article while also retaining that article's "live" appearance (e.g., hyperlinks still appear in blue font, headings are present, citations appear as bracketed footnotes, templates are rendered in full). For many, the Visual Editor has been a godsend that spares contributors from wading through complex jumbles of wikitext just to fix a typo.

You can use the Visual Editor on most Wikipedia pages, but note that it is permanently disabled when working on talk pages. This means that wikitext markup still has a place, and we will cover it in greater detail in chapter 4.

To edit using the Visual Editor, go to an article you want to amend and click the **Edit** button in the top-right corner of the screen; alternatively, you can go to a subsection of an article and click the **Edit** button next to the section heading. The Visual Editor is usually on by default for new users, but if you click the Edit button and find yourself redirected to the scary wikitext editor (described in chapter 4), you will need to switch to the Visual Editor by hand. To do this, click on the pencil icon (✐) in the upper right-hand corner of the editor screen and choose **Switch to the Visual Editor**. This will redirect you to the Visual Editor view of the article. At the top of the article, you should now see a **Visual Editor toolbar** (fig. 3.2). With this toolbar you can format text, add citations, create links, and much more.

Figure 3.2. A Look at the Visual Editor

Table 3.3. Elements of the Visual Editor

Label	Feature	Icon	Description
A	"Undo" and "Redo" buttons	↶ ↷	The "Undo" button (*left*) will reverse the last edit you made, whereas the "Redo" button (*right*) will restore your last edit.
B	"Format paragraph" button		This opens a drop-down menu that allows you to apply preset formatting to text. (This menu is similar to Microsoft Word's "Styles" options).
C	"Style text" button	*A*	This opens a drop-down menu that allows you to make selected text italic or bold.
D	"Link" button	∞	This button will open the **Add a link** window, which allows you to insert and adjust wikilinks or external links.
E	"Cite" button	66	This button will open the **Add a Citation** window, which allows you to insert and adjust Wikipedia-generated citational templates.
F	"Structure" button	≔	This opens a drop-down menu allowing you to create bulleted/numbered lists, or increase/decrease indentation of the article's text.
G	"Insert" button		This enables you to add images, templates, tables, and many other graphic features.
H	"Special characters" button	Ω	This opens a collection of specialized characters and symbols that can be inserted into an article.
I	"Help" button	?	This button will open a window, through which you can access a user guide, or display a list of keyboard shortcuts.
J	"Page options" button	≡	This opens a drop-down menu of features that allow you to adjust how the article is displayed.
K	"Switch editor" tab	✏	With this button, you can switch between the plain text editor and the visual editor.
L	"Publish changes . . ." button		Clicking this saves any changes you have made to the article, updating it for the whole world to see.

If you want to always open articles with the Visual Editor, bypassing the source editor in the process, you may need to adjust your editing preferences. To do this:

1. Click the **Preferences** link in your user options toolbar in the upper right-hand corner of the screen.
2. Once on the Preferences page, click the tab that says **Editing**.
3. Navigate to the section titled **Editing mode**. Immediately below this title is a drop-down menu.
4. From this menu, choose the option **Always give the visual editor if possible**.
5. Click the **Save** button at the bottom of the page.

The drop-down menu in the Editing tab also gives you the option to work only with the source editor, or to have both editors available to you at the same time. If you find yourself unhappy with the setting that you picked, you can always switch to a different one.

Formatting Text

Now we are ready to take the Visual Editor for a spin. Let's start by doing something simple, such as italicizing or bolding text. To do this:

1. Open the article you want to edit and switch to the Visual Editor.
2. Somewhere in the article, either type out new text *or* select existing text.
3. From the Visual Editor Toolbar, click the **Style** (**A**) button (fig. 3.3a).

This will open a drop-down menu. Here, you have three main options:

 a. If you want to make the text bold, click on the **Bold** option (fig. 3.3b).
 b. If you want to italicize the text, click on the **Italic** option (fig. 3.3c).
 c. If you want to remove any formatting, click **More** (fig. 3.3d) and choose the option **Remove**.

4. As soon as you choose your format preference, the editor will refresh the article, reflecting in real time how your edit impacts the look of the page.
5. To update the page and lock in your changes, click **Publish changes** . . . and add an **Edit summary**. Then click **Publish changes** . . . once more.

Note that during step 4, you can also click **More** (fig. 3.3d). Doing so will display a few more formatting options that, among other things, allow you to strike through text, create subscript and superscript fonts, and insert computer code. (The average Wikipedia editor, however, is unlikely to use these options on a regular basis.)

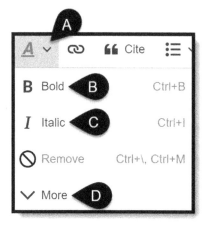

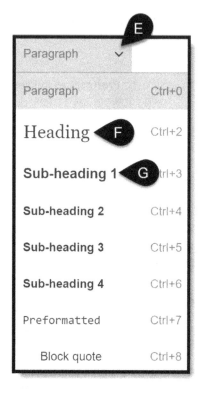

Figure 3.3. Tools for Formatting Text

Adding Section Headings

To make Wikipedia articles easier to navigate, they are often divided into discrete sections, visually demarcated by heading levels. If an article includes more than three first-level section headings, a table of contents will automatically load just after the article's introductory paragraph(s). This table of contents will list the names of article sections and provide a wikilink to each section. This means that a reader can click on a heading in the table of contents and jump right to that section without scrolling through the entire article. When creating your own section headings, it is important to remember that they need to be written in sentence case, meaning that only the first word of the heading and any proper nouns are capitalized. (In other words, your headings should look `Something like this`, rather than `Something Like This`). To add section headings using the Visual Editor:

1. Open the article you wish to edit in the Visual Editor.
2. Place your cursor on a new line and type a new heading in sentence case.

Chapter 3

3. Next, highlight the text you have just written. Then, from the Visual Editor toolbar, select the **Paragraph** drop-down button (fig. 3.3e).
4. Choose which heading level you want to create. In this example, I want it to be a primary heading, so I will choose **Heading** (fig. 3.3f).
5. As soon as you choose your level, the editor will refresh the text's appearance, and you should now see your text rendered as a heading.
6. Publish your changes and add an Edit summary.

If you want to create a subheading, simply repeat these steps, but change which heading level you choose during step 4 (e.g., if you want to create a subheading, choose **Sub-heading 1**, etc. [fig. 3.3g] from the drop-down button).

Adding Links

A wikilink is the term for the many hyperlinks on the site that, when clicked, send a reader to another article. Most wikilinks appear as blue hyperlinks, but if the destination page to which a wikilink points does not yet exist, the hyperlink will

Figure 3.4. How to Insert a Wikilink

be red (in other words, these pages are under construction). Wikilinks are among the most important elements of Wikipedia, as they connect the site's millions of articles to one another, resulting in a complex informational rhizome with no center or master index. To add a wikilink to an article using the Visual Editor:

1. Open the article you wish to edit in the Visual Editor.
2. Select text that you want to link to another Wikipedia page (fig. 3.4a).
3. From the Visual Editor toolbar, click the **Link** (∞) button (fig. 3.4b). This will open the "Add a link" pop-up box (fig. 3.4c).
4. Type the name of the target article in the space provided (fig. 3.4d). Do not worry if the text that you have selected is a bit different from the actual name of an article.
5. When you locate the right article, click on it (fig. 3.4e); this will format the selected text automatically, turning it into a wikilink.
6. Publish your changes and add an Edit summary.

Adding External Links

Most of the links that you add into Wikipedia will be to other articles. However, sometimes, when you are editing an article's "External links" section, you might need to add a hyperlink that leads to an off-site resource. To do this:

1. Open the article or article section you wish to edit in the Visual Editor.
2. Select text that you want to link to an external Web page (fig. 3.5a).

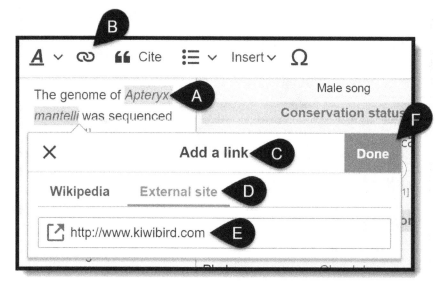

Figure 3.5. How to Insert an External Link

3. From the Visual Editor toolbar, select the **Link** (⌘) button (fig. 3.5b). This will open the "Add a link" pop-up box (fig. 3.5c), which by default lands on the Wikipedia tab.
4. Click the tab that reads **External site** (fig. 3.5d). In this tab, type or paste the URL of the website to which you want to link (fig. 3.5e).
5. When the link is recognized, click **Done** (fig. 3.5f).
6. Publish your changes and add an Edit summary.

Adding Citations

Another aspect of Wikipedia integral to its identity as a reference source is its use of citations (also called "references," or "refs," by editors). According to the site's manual of style, every statement on Wikipedia—with some exceptions— needs to be backed up with a reliable citation. In the body of the text, a Wikipedia citation will appear as a numbered, superscript footnote. When you click on a footnote, you will be forwarded to the bottom of the article, where the full bibliographic details of the source will be displayed, alongside any other citations used on the page, in a dedicated reference section. To add a citation to an article:

1. Open the article you wish to edit in the Visual Editor.
2. Place your cursor where you want to generate a reference (fig. 3.6a). Remember that on Wikipedia, citations immediately follow punctuation marks such as periods and commas, without any spaces in between.

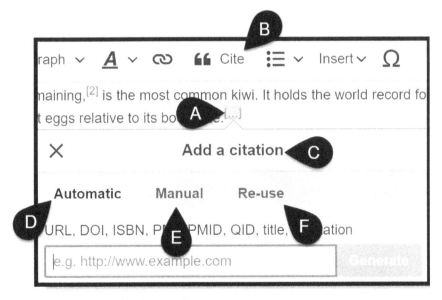

Figure 3.6. How to Add a Citation (Part 1)

3. Click the **Cite** (❝❞) button (fig. 3.6b). This will open the "Add a citation" pop-up box (fig. 3.6c).

From here, you can generate a citation a few different ways: you can use an identifier like an ISBN number to generate the citation (fig. 3.6d), you can manually cite the citation (fig. 3.6e), or you can reuse a citation that is already in the article (fig. 3.6f). Let's take a closer look at each of these methods.

AUTOMATICALLY GENERATING A CITATION

Automatically generating a citation is the easiest method to insert a reference, but it requires you to provide a "clue" so that the Visual Editor can track down the pertinent information. The identifying "clues" that work with this tool include:

- **URLs**—A uniform resource locator; this is better known as a Web address (e.g., https://www.nytimes.com/ or https://www.bbc.com/).
- **DOIs**—A "digital object identifier," used to identify and track scholarly publications such as journal articles or monographs. DOIs are usually a jumble of numbers, letters, and punctuation marks (e.g., 10.1901/jaba.1974.7-497a).
- **ISBNs**—An "international standard book number"; the code of ten or thirteen numbers that appears on the barcode of a book and its copyright page (e.g., 9780898156126 or 9780981679266).
- **PMIDs**—A "PubMed identifier"; a string of numbers used to identify articles in the PubMed medical database (e.g., 24312205).
- **QIDs**—A "Q-identifier"; a number used by the Wikidata project to catalog "any kind of topic, concept, or object"[7] (e.g., "Q42" links to the author Douglas Adams).
- **Titles**—The title of the work that you want to cite.

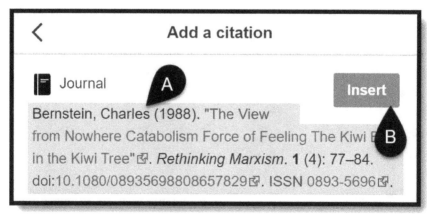

Figure 3.7. How to Add a Citation (Part 2)

Once you drop in your clue of choice, select **Generate** from the "Add a citation" pop-up box; this will redirect you to a page with a potential list of citations (fig. 3.7a). If you see the one you want, click the **Insert** button (fig. 3.7b), and the reference will be added to the article.

MANUALLY CREATING A CITATION

Sometimes you will not be able to generate a citation automatically. In that case, you can use the "Manual" option to type a citation by hand. To do this:

1. Follow steps 1–3 from "Adding Citations" (pp. 55–56).
2. From the "Add a citation" window, select **Manual** (fig. 3.8a), then choose which reference type you want to work with; the main four options are:
   a. "Website" (⬛),
   b. "Newspaper" (⬛),
   c. "Book" (⬛), and
   d. "Journal article" (⬛) (fig. 3.8b).
   You can also click the "Basic" (⬛) option (fig. 3.8c), which will provide a blank reference template to work with.
3. Once you have selected your reference type, the Visual Editor will redirect you to a form (fig. 3.8d), which you will need to fill out by adding pertinent bibliographic information (fig. 3.8e).
4. When you have entered everything, click the **Insert** button (fig. 3.8f) at the top of the screen.
5. Publish your changes and add an Edit summary.

REUSING A CITATION

What if you are working on an article and you find yourself repeatedly citing a single source? If you create a new numbered footnote every time you cite that resource, your reference section will soon overflow with duplicates. Thankfully, Wikipedia allows you to cut down on this redundancy by citing a single reference multiple times in an article. To do this:

1. Follow steps 1–3 from "Adding Citations" (pp. 55–56).
2. From the "Add a citation" window, select the **Re-use** tab (fig. 3.9a). This will bring up a list of all the citations currently being used in the article.
3. Scan the list for the citation you need. You can also type in a keyword, phrase, author name, and so forth in the search bar (fig. 3.9b) to narrow your selection.
4. When you find the citation that you want to reuse (fig. 3.9c), simply click on it, and Wikipedia will take care of the rest.
5. Publish your changes and add an Edit summary.

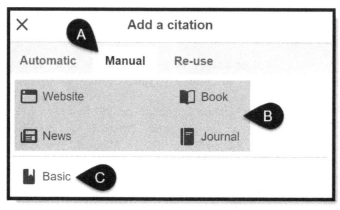

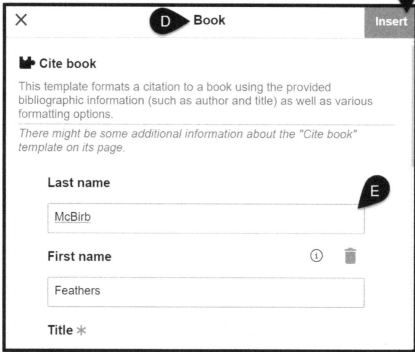

Figure 3.8. How to Manually Create a Citation

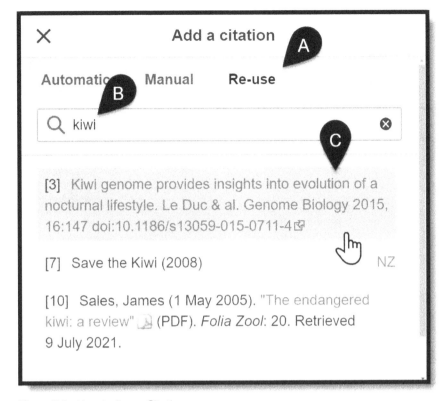

Figure 3.9. How to Reuse Citations

EDITING A CITATION

What if you need to edit a citation already added to an article? Don't worry! The Visual Editor has you covered. To adjust a citation, simply:

1. Click on the footnote marker of the citation you want to edit (fig. 3.10a); a small pop-up window will appear showing you how the full reference is currently being rendered (fig. 3.10b).
2. Click **Edit** (fig. 3.10c).
3. This will bring you to the template for whatever citation type you are adjusting (fig. 3.10d). Fill in, delete, or adjust the fields as necessary (fig. 3.10e).
4. Click **Apply Changes** (fig. 3.10f).
5. Publish your changes and add an Edit summary.

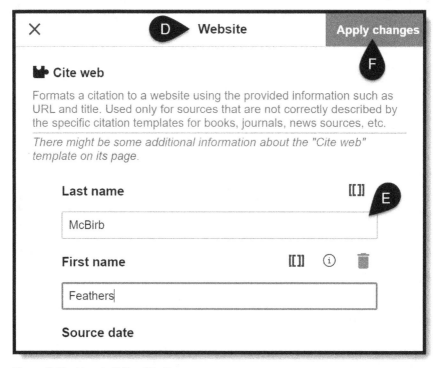

Figure 3.10. How to Edit a Citation

ADDING A REFERENCE LIST TO AN ARTICLE

As mentioned at the start of this section, every article should have a reference list at the bottom of the page. This reference list functions like a corral for all the citations that appear in an article, grouping them together in one easily accessible place. Citations in a reference list appear in the order that they are cited within the article. To add a reference list to an article:

1. Open the article you wish to edit in the Visual Editor.
2. Place your cursor near the end of the article (right after the "See also" section, but before the "External links" section or any navigation boxes, if present).

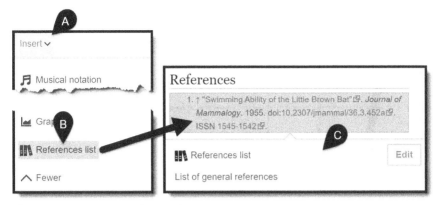

Figure 3.11. Inserting a Reference List

3. On a new line, type a title for your reference list; something like "References" or "Works cited" is generally preferred. Highlight your title, click the **Paragraph** drop-down menu from the toolbar, and click **Heading**.
4. Hit Enter/Return to jump to a new line.
5. Click **Insert** (fig. 3.11a) from the toolbar and choose **More**.
6. Scroll down and select the **References list** (📖) option (fig. 3.11b). This will drop a dynamic list into your article (fig. 3.11c) that will grow and shrink, depending on whether citations are added or removed from the article.
7. Publish your changes and add an Edit summary.

Adding Images

When I work with students to create new Wikipedia pages, often one of the first things they want to do is add images to their articles. It is an understandable impulse, as images can make an otherwise boring page really pop. The problem is that most images found online cannot be reused without permission of the copyright holder(s). Because Wikipedia is a free resource that can be reused freely even in commercial projects, the site cannot host copyrighted material without permission of the rights holder(s). Luckily, the Wikimedia Foundation established the Wikimedia Commons to house thousands of free images that can be used on Wikipedia without worry about copyright violation. Even better, you can use the Visual Editor to search through what the Commons has to offer. To add a free image to an article using the Visual Editor, follow these steps:

1. Open the article or article section you wish to edit in the Visual Editor.
2. Place your cursor where you want an image to go. (Note that images should be placed between paragraphs, not in the middle of text.)

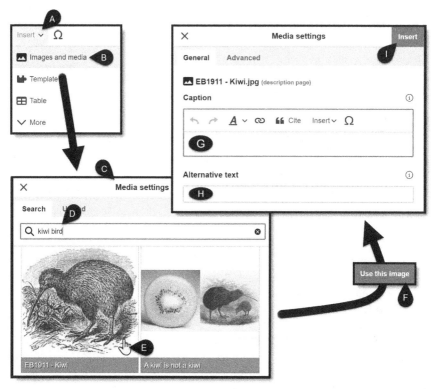

Figure 3.12. Adding an Image to an Article

3. Click the **Insert** drop-down option (fig. 3.12a) from the Visual Editor toolbar.
4. From the options listed, choose **Images and media** (▨) (fig. 3.12b).
5. A Wikimedia search window will appear (fig. 3.12c); type a keyword or phrase to look for a suitable image (fig. 3.12d).
6. Once you have found the image you want, click on it (fig. 3.12e). You will be asked if you want to **Use this Image** (fig. 3.12f).
7. This will redirect you to a box that asks you to provide a caption for the image (fig. 3.12g) and alternative text (fig. 3.12h) (to better understand alternative text, see "Accessibility Considerations" in chapter 5).
8. Click **Insert** (fig. 3.12i). This will add the image to the article.
9. Publish your changes and add an Edit summary.

If you want to upload your own images, flip to the "Uploading Images" section in chapter 5, which explains how to upload images to Wikimedia Commons yourself.

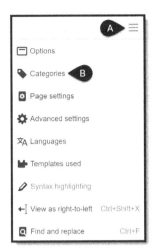
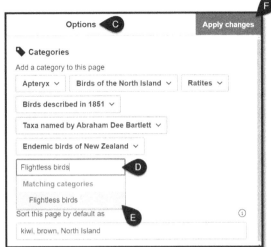

Figure 3.13. Adding an Article to a Category

Categorizing Articles

To make it easier for readers to find articles related to one another, Wikipedia pages are often grouped by category tags. These tags (which look like specialized hyperlinks) are located at the very bottom of an article in a dark gray box. Clicking on one of these links takes the reader to an alphabetical list of all the articles that share that category tag. To add an article to a category with the Visual Editor:

1. Open the article you wish to edit in the Visual Editor.
2. Click the **Page options button** (≡) (fig. 3.13a); from the drop-down list, select **Categories** (🏷) (fig. 3.13b).
3. This will take you to the "Categories" section of the "Options" tab (fig. 3.13c).
4. In the search bar that says "Add a category" in gray text (fig. 3.13d), search for existing categories by typing pertinent keywords.
5. When you find a matching category, click on it (fig. 3.13e), which will add the article to that category.
6. When you are finished, click **Apply changes** (fig. 3.13f).
7. Publish your changes and add an Edit summary. When back in "Read" mode, you will see the category hyperlinked at the bottom of the article.

Working with Templates

A "Wikipedia template" is an element that can be consistently and repeatedly used across multiple articles (a process referred to as transclusion). Examples of Wikipedia templates include citation templates, as well as the infobox and the navigation box elements mentioned earlier in the "Anatomy of a Wikipedia Article" section. Templates work by taking textual/formatting cues from a source, then dropping these cues into the article you are editing. Most templates have fields that can be manipulated, allowing editors to tailor a template to suit the needs of the articles that they are working on. This means that editors can use the same templates across a bevy of articles, without having to re-create every detail by hand.

Almost every Wikipedia article will have a template somewhere in the text. John Broughton argues that the popularity of Wikipedia templates is due to the way they help ensure consistency, save editors' time, and keep pages updated automatically.[8] Having said all of this, templates can be among Wikipedia's trickiest features;[9] personally, if you want to work with them, I believe it is best

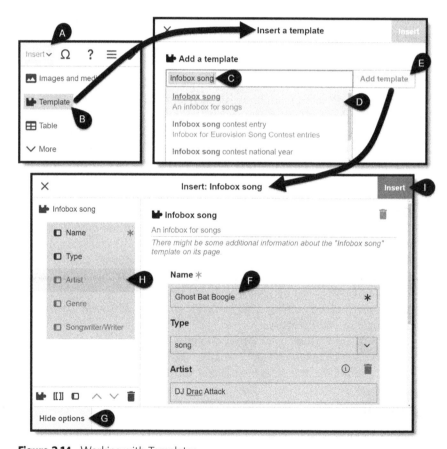

Figure 3.14. Working with Templates

to use the wikitext editor so you can see all the nitty-gritty details. Nevertheless, they can still be added to articles with the Visual Editor. To do this:

1. Open the article or article section you wish to edit in the Visual Editor.
2. Click the **Insert** button (fig. 3.14a); from the drop-down list, select **Templates** (📽️) (fig. 3.14b). This will open the "Insert a template" pop-up box.
3. In the search bar under the "Add a template" header, type the name of the template you want to use (fig. 3.14c). The drop-down will then list possible templates.
4. When you see the template listed that you want to use (fig. 3.14d), select it and click the **Add template** button (fig. 3.14e).
5. This will redirect you to the "Insert: Template" pop-up box. Template fields that you will need to fill out will be on the right of the screen (fig. 3.14f).
6. You can also click the **Show/Hide Options** button (fig. 3.14g) in the lower left-hand side of the box to display an outline of the template you are working with (fig. 3.14h).
7. When you are finished adding or editing the fields, click **Insert**. Once you save the article, the template will be loaded into the article and automatically formatted accordingly.
8. When you are satisfied, publish your changes and add an Edit summary.

CREATING ARTICLES

If you are a brand-new editor still getting a feel for the website, you will be required to create articles via the Wikipedia:Articles for creation portal. On this page, the **Click here to start a new article** link enables you to create a draft for a new page. When you are satisfied with the way your draft looks and reads, you can submit it for review. A more seasoned editor will then check to see whether the article is of quality. If your article passes the quality test, it goes live; if not, it remains a draft, and you can try again.

Wikipedia:Articles for creation is, in theory, a solid idea to ensure the quality of new pages. Unfortunately, the process can very easily get backlogged, and it can take weeks, if not months, before a draft is reviewed. Often, a quicker way to create an article is to whip up a draft and then move it to Wikipedia's mainspace. Note that this will require you to have been an editor for at least four days and to have made at least ten edits, so plan accordingly. To create a draft and move it:

1. Make sure that the article you want to create does not already exist on Wikipedia. This may require you to perform a few creative searches to see what is out there: for instance, although it is true that (as of 2021) a search for "Former Spanish colonies in the Asia-Pacific region" does not turn up an article with that exact name, an article about that topic does

exist at <u>Spanish East Indies</u>. Creating a new <u>Former Spanish colonies in the Asia-Pacific region</u> article would, therefore, be redundant.

2. If you cannot find an article on a topic that you believe Wikipedia should cover, navigate to <u>Wikipedia:Article_wizard/CreateDraft</u>.

3. Place your cursor in the **Enter your draft name here** slot and type the name of the article that you want to create. Remember, Wikipedia uses sentence case for its titles, so the name you give your article should look <u>Like this</u> (and <u>Not Like This</u>).

4. Switch to the Visual Editor (if necessary) and create a draft article using the processes discussed in this chapter. For a more detailed discussion of how a standard article should be laid out, see <u>Wikipedia:Manual of Style/ Layout</u>.

5. When you are satisfied with what you have made, publish your changes and add an Edit summary.

And just like that, your work has been published as a draft. The final step is to move your draft to Wikipedia's mainspace (that is, the forward-facing part of the website where articles are most easily accessible to readers). This will require us to **Rename** the article. To do this:

1. Go to your draft article (if necessary, search for it by typing `Draft:` followed immediately by the title, e.g., `Draft:Like this`). On the draft

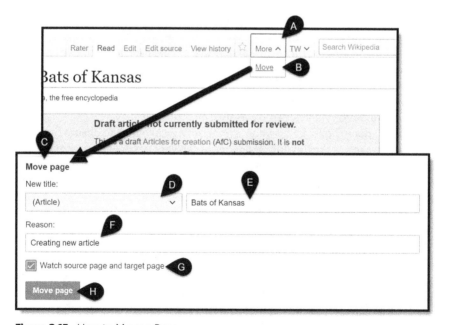

Figure 3.15. How to Move a Page

page, go to the upper right-hand corner of the screen and click **More** (fig. 3.15a).

2. From this drop-down menu, select **Move** (fig. 3.15b). This will take you to the **Move page** form (fig. 3.15c).
3. From the drop-down menu under **New title**, switch **Draft** to **(Article)** (fig. 3.15d).
4. In the box next to the drop-down menu, type in the intended name of your article. For instance, if I were creating an article about the bats of Kansas, I would enter `Bats of Kansas` (fig. 3.15e).
5. In the **Reason** box, type something like "Creating new article" (fig. 3.15f).
6. You can choose to add this article to your Watchlist by checking the **Watch source page and target page** box (fig. 3.15g).
7. Finally, click **Move page** (fig. 3.15h). This will move the article from draft space onto the mainspace of Wikipedia.

Checking History Pages

Some people do not realize that although Wikipedia pages are constantly being edited, the site archives every iteration of an article. These page iterations, or "revisions," are accessible to any user—registered or not—by clicking on the **View History** tab in the upper right-hand corner of an article: the **History** page logs every edit made to an article, in chronological order, stretching back to when the article was created. The History page also lists which editors made the edits, how big those edits were, and when they were made. Let's take a quick look at the various features of an article's History tab:

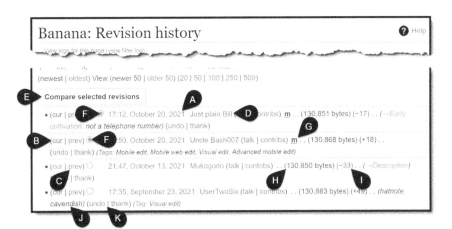

Figure 3.16. A Look at the History Page

Table 3.4. Elements of the History Tab

Label	Feature	Description
A	Link to revision	This hyperlink will take you to a snapshot of the article, illustrating how the page looked at the time a specific edit was made. This snapshot also records the date and time of the edit.
B	Current revision comparison	This will compare the current version of the article with the selected revision.
C	Previous revision comparison	This will compare a selected revision to the one that preceded it.
D	User name	This identifies the editor responsible for a revision.
E	Compare selected revisions button	This button will compare two different revisions from the article's history. To select which revisions to compare, you will need to use the circular revision selectors (F).
F	Revision selectors	Filling these selectors will tell Wikipedia which revisions you would like to contrast when clicking the *Compare selected revision button* (E). You can only compare two revisions at a time.
G	Minor edit notice	This means that the edit in question was a minor (i.e., small) one.
H	Byte size of article	This is the size of the article, in bytes, after an edit was made.
I	Change in byte size	This tells you how many bytes were added or removed during an edit, or if the size of the article stayed the same. Digits indicating addition are in green and are preceded by a plus (+) sign; digits indicating subtraction are in red and are preceded by a minus (–) sign.
J	Edit summary	This displays the edit summary left by an editor after they have made an edit to the page.
K	Undo	Undoes the selected edit.

The "Undo" feature is arguably one of the more useful features found on the History tab, as it enables editors to quickly and easily undo (or "revert") edits that are unproductive, fallacious, or disruptive. If you plan to fight off vandals, the "Undo" button likely will become your best friend.

4

Growing as an Editor

To Wikitext and Beyond

As you spend more time editing articles, you likely will start to work on projects that require an increasing amount of Wiki-know-how. To better prepare you for these sorts of challenges, the present chapter moves beyond the capabilities of the Visual Editor and formally introduces "wikitext," or the unique syntax that Wikipedia uses to code and format its articles.

Although it can be confusing at first, wikitext markup is worth learning, as it is the only way you can communicate with other editors on talk pages and the like; it also allows for greater precision when editing, given that you are working on the source level. After a discussion of wikitext's technical details, I consider ways that you can peer-review articles, submit pages for "good article" assessment, or promote articles to "featured" status. I then turn to the scandalous topic of vandalism by exploring the ways articles are protected from vandals and the processes, if necessary, by which articles are deleted. I close the chapter with a discussion of "WikiProjects," or groups of editors organized around a given topic. To my eye, these projects exemplify the spirit of Wiki-teamwork, proving that with enough editors and the right amount of dedication, no editing project is too large.

EDITING WITH WIKITEXT

Wikitext refers to the source text and the markup coding that tells the site exactly how an article should be formatted when being viewed in "read" mode; logically, it is by modifying this markup an editor can directly impact the look of an article. Unfortunately, despite being the most direct method of editing, working with wikitext can at times be complicated and frustrating, especially if you are not familiar with the basics of hypertext markup. Nevertheless, developing a basic understanding of wikitext is critical if you want to grow as an editor, given that the Visual Editor is not available for use on talk pages. This means that if you stick with only the Visual Editor, you will not be able to reach out to other editors, coordinate your efforts, or jump into discussions to share your thoughts.

Given the importance of wikitext, the first part of this chapter will focus on demystifying the secrets of the site's markup language.

Let's begin by queuing up the wikitext editor. Go to the top of an article and click on the tab that reads **Edit**; this will open the Visual Editor, which we discussed in chapter 3. To switch to the wikitext editor, click on the pencil icon (✏️) in the upper right-hand corner of the screen and choose the option that says **Source editing**. You will then be redirected to a new edit screen that looks something like what you see in figure 4.1. This is the "source editor" or "wikitext editor" screen, the features of which have been annotated in table 4.1:

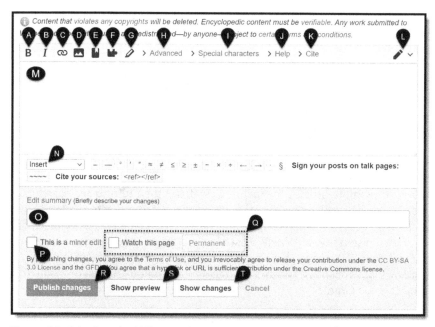

Figure 4.1. A Look at the Wikitext Editor

Table 4.1. Elements of the Wikitext Editor

Label	Feature	Icon	Description
A	"Bold" button	**B**	Selecting text in the edit screen (M) and then clicking this button will tell the site to display that text in bold.
B	"Italic" button	*I*	Selecting text in the edit screen (M) and then clicking this button will tell the site to display that text in italics.
C	"Link" button	∞	This button will open the **Insert link** window, which allows you to insert and adjust wikilinks.
D	"Images and media" button	▨	This button will open the **Insert file** window, which you can use to insert images into an article.
E	"Reference" button	▊	Selecting text in the edit screen (M) and then clicking this button will place `<ref> </ref>` tags around that text. These tags tell Wikipedia to treat the bracketed text as a reference.
F	"Insert a template" button	▚	This will open a search window that enables you to search for and insert Wikipedia templates.
G	"Syntax highlighting" button	⟋	When activated, this feature will alert you to the presence of wiki-markup by underlining text and/or changing font color and size.
H	"Advanced" tab		This opens the "Advanced" tab, which is explicated later in this chapter.
I	"Special characters" tab		This opens a collection of specialized characters and symbols that can be inserted into an article.
J	"Help" tab		This displays a "cheat sheet" outlining the basics of wikitext markup. (A similar outline is included at the end of this chapter.)
K	"Cite" tab		This tool enables an editor to generate citational templates, repeat named citations, or check for citation errors.
L	"Switch editor" tab	✎	With this button, you can switch between the plain text editor and the Visual Editor.
M	Edit screen		This is the area in which you make edits.
N	"Insert" drop-down menu		Similar to the "Special characters" tab, this drop-down menu provides access to navigable lists of special characters and symbols. It also contains a list of relevant markup codes.

(continued)

Table 4.1. (*continued*)

Label	Feature	Icon	Description
O	"Edit summary" text box		This is where you summarize any changes that you have made to an article. Leaving an edit summary is not required, but it is considered good wiki-etiquette.
P	"This is a minor edit" check box		Checking this box will log an edit as "minor, " meaning that it is a superficial change (e.g., fixing a typo, adding missing punctuation).
Q	"Watch this page" option		Checking this box will add the present article to your Watchlist; the drop-down menu specifies how long you want the article to remain on your list.
R	"Publish page" button		Clicking this button will update the article with any changes you have made.
S	"Show preview" button		Clicking this button will show you a preview of how your edits might impact the look of the article. Editors can use this to review their changes before they commit to saving them.
T	"Show changes" button		Clicking this button will compare any changes you have made to an article with the last saved revision of that article.

The Advanced Tab

Clicking on the "Advanced" tab in the wikitext editor opens a whole new world of tools that make formatting articles easier. The major features of this tab are as follows:

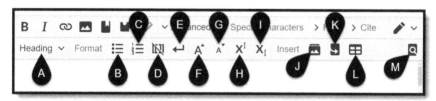

Figure 4.2. The Wikitext Editor's Advanced Tab

Table 4.2. The Wikitext Editor's Advanced Tab

Label	Feature	Icons	Description
A	"Heading" drop-down list		Clicking this tells the site to treat selected text as second, third, fourth, or fifth-level headings.
B	"Bulleted list" button	☰	Selecting text in the edit screen and then clicking this button will tell the site to display that text as a bulleted list.
C	"Numbered list" button	☷	Selecting text in the edit screen and then clicking this button will tell the site to display that text as an enumerated list.
D	"No wiki formatting" button	🚫	This will place <nowiki></nowiki> tags around selected text in the edit screen. This tells Wikipedia to ignore any wiki-markup within the confines of the tags.
E	"New line" button	↵	This inserts the code into the text, which functions as a line break.
F	"Big" button	A˙	This will place <big></big> tags around selected text in the edit screen. This tells Wikipedia to render the text in a larger script.
G	"Small" button	A˙	This will place <small></small> tags around selected text in the edit screen. This tells Wikipedia to render the text in a smaller script.
H	"Superscript" button	X^I	This will place tags around selected text in the edit screen. This tells Wikipedia to render the text in superscript.
I	"Subscript" button	X_I	This will place tags around selected text in the edit screen. This tells Wikipedia to render the text in subscript.
J	"Insert Picture Gallery" button	🖼	You can use this tool to insert a picture gallery into an article.
K	"Insert Redirect" button	⬛	This will insert #REDIRECT Target page name into the article. Replacing Target page name with the name of a different article will redirect readers to that article any time they wikilink to this article.
L	"Insert Table" button	⊞	This will insert a table into the article.
M	"Search and replace" button	🔍	This tool allows an editor to search for one keyword or phrase and replace it with another.

Formatting Text, Previewing Your Edit, and Saving Changes

To add content using the wikitext editor, place your cursor in the big white box that takes up most of the screen and begin typing. It is important to remember that the wikitext editor renders everything in plain text, meaning that if you want to format words, phrases, and so forth, you will need to code this formatting using wikitext. Some basic formatting tasks are outlined in the following table:

Table 4.3. Formatting Text with the Wikitext Editor

Formatting Element	How to Add Using the Wikitext Editor	Example Wikitext View	Example Published View
Bold Text	Select pertinent text and click the **Bold** button (fig. 4.1a), *or* you can surround the text with three straight apostrophes.	`'''This is bold text.'''`	**This is bold text.**
Italic Text	Select pertinent text and click the **Italic** button (fig. 4.1b), *or* you can surround the text with two straight apostrophes.	`''This is italicized text.''`	*This is italicized text.*
Bold and Italic Text	Select pertinent text and click both the **Bold** and **Italic** buttons (figs. 4.1a–b), *or* you can surround the text with five straight apostrophes.	`'''''This is bold and italicized text.'''''`	***This is bold and italicized text.***

Bulleted List	Begin on a new line and type an asterisk, followed by the first line of the list. To add subsequent entries, hit enter and repeat the steps.	`* Entry 1`
		`* Entry 2`
		`* Entry 3`
			• Entry 1
			• Entry 2
			• Entry 3

Numbered List	Begin on a new line and type a hash sign, followed by the first line of the list. To add subsequent entries, hit enter and repeat the steps.	`# Entry number 1`
		`# Entry number 2`
		`# Entry number 3`
			1. Entry number 1
			2. Entry number 2
			3. Entry number 3

If you want to see how your edits will impact the article, click the **Show preview** button near the bottom of the editor window. (This is a great tool for catching typos or errors before you make revisions public.) If you are satisfied with how things look and wish to save your changes, scroll to the bottom of the editor screen and select the option that reads **Publish changes**. This will redirect you to a new "Read" view of the article, updated to reflect your contributions.

Adding Wikilinks

You can add a wikilink to an article in several ways. For beginners, the easiest method is to use the "Insert link" feature accessible from the editor toolbar. To use this tool:

1. Navigate to an article, and click **Edit source**. In the editor, type or select the word/phrase that you want to wikilink (fig. 4.3a).
2. Select the **Insert link** (🔗) button from the edit toolbar (fig. 4.3b). This will open the **Insert link** (fig. 4.3c) window.
3. In the **Target page or URL** slot, type the exact name of the destination Wikipedia article (fig. 4.3d). Wikipedia will automatically list possible articles as you type; clicking on one of these suggestions will autofill the slot. The window will also let you know if the destination article exists (fig. 4.3e).

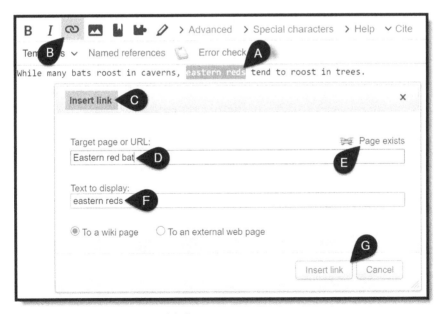

Figure 4.3. How to Insert a Wikilink

4. In the **Text to display** slot, enter the way you want the wikilink to be displayed in Read mode (fig. 4.3f). This is useful when linking to articles with disambiguating parentheticals that might otherwise look awkward spelled out in full, or when the exact title of an article does not fit into the syntax of a sentence. (When a wikilink's display text does not match the title of the destination article, the wikilink is referred to as a "piped link.")
5. When you have selected the appropriate article and adjusted the display text, click **Insert link** (fig. 4.3g).
6. Add an **Edit summary** and click **Submit changes** to update the article.

ADDING WIKILINKS BY HAND

It is not uncommon for Wikipedia editors to eventually forgo the "Insert link" tool and instead begin to edit wikilinks into articles by hand. This is done by manually enclosing a word or phrase in double square brackets; for instance, amending an article by adding in `[[Grapevine beetle]]` would result in a wikilink to the article about the Grapevine beetle species. When manually creating a piped link, however, you will need to type the full title of the article to which you want to link, and immediately follow with a vertical bar (| , which can be inserted by typing Shift+\) and the text that you want displayed. You will then surround the entire construction in double square brackets. The end result will look something like this: `[[Article title|text to be displayed]]`.

Here is a more coherent example: Suppose I edit into an article the following sentence: `The flying fox is a type of bat that eats fruit.` Now let's say that I want to link the phrases "flying fox" and "eats fruits" to the articles Flying fox and Frugivore, respectively. In the case of the former, the article name matches the text in my sentence, so all I have to do is surround the words "flying fox" with square brackets: `The [[flying fox]] is a type of bat that eats fruit.` Linking to the Frugivore article is a little trickier, because I did not use that exact term in my sentence. I will thus have to pipe in the link. To do this, I will first type the name of the destination article (`Frugivore`), followed immediately by a vertical bar (|). I will then type the text that I want displayed in the article (`eats fruit`) before surrounding the entire construction in double brackets. The final sentence, written in proper wikitext, should read as follows: `The [[flying fox]] is a type of bat that [[Frugivore|eats fruit]].`

ADDING EXTERNAL LINKS

To add an off-site link in the "External links" section of an article, type the full target URL and surround it in single square brackets: `[http://www.example.org]`. When you save your edit, the external link will be displayed as a bracketed number followed by the external link icon: [1] ↗.

If you want the link also to include a text label, type out the full URL, add a space, and then type the text that you want displayed. Enclose this entire construction in single square brackets so that it looks like this: `[http://www.example.org Example text]`. When you save the article, the external link will appear as a blue hyperlink followed by the external link icon: Example text 🗗.

Adding References

As was discussed in chapter 3, references are perhaps the most important part of a Wikipedia article. The simplest way to add in a reference through the wikitext editor is to use the "Reference" button in the toolbar:

1. Navigate to an article and click **Edit source**. In the text editor, place your cursor where you want to generate a citation (fig. 4.4a); remember that on Wikipedia, citations immediately follow punctuation marks such as periods and commas, without any spaces in between.
2. Type out what you want your reference entry to say, highlight that text (fig. 4.4b), and then click on the **Reference** (📑) button (fig. 4.4c). This will place `<ref>` `</ref>` tags around your text (fig. 4.4d). These are the citation tags, and they tell Wikipedia that the text between them is to be treated as a reference; they also tell Wikipedia where to generate an enumerated footnote marker.
3. Scroll to the bottom of the article and make sure that it includes the reference template `{{Reflist}}`. This template tells Wikipedia where to display an article's references in full. If the article lacks this template, add it to the bottom of the page (fig. 4.4e).
4. Add an **Edit summary** and click **Submit changes**.
5. Once the article is published, you will now see that a footnote appears where you added the citation (fig. 4.4f); clicking on this footnote will take

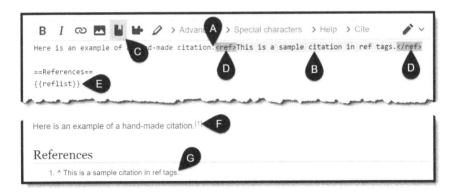

Figure 4.4. How to Create a Simple Citation

you to the bottom of the page, where the reference, in full, will be listed (fig. 4.4g).

ADDING A REFERENCE USING REFTOOLBAR TEMPLATES

Editors also have the option to create references using RefToolbar. This feature generates citation templates, with fields that editors can fill out. When editors save, the template is transformed into a consistently formatted reference. To create a citation with RefToolbar:

1. Navigate to an article and click **Edit source**. In the wikitext editor, place your cursor where you want to generate a citation (fig. 4.5a).
2. From the editor options, click on the tab that says **Cite** (fig. 4.5b).
3. Hover over the tab that says **Templates** (fig. 4.5c) and choose the type of reference you want to cite (fig. 4.5d). The options here are for a website (**cite web**), a newspaper (**cite news**), a book (**cite book**), or an academic journal article (**cite journal**).
4. Clicking on a template will open the RefToolbar window (fig. 4.5e), which will display the necessary fields for the citation type that you selected.
5. Fill out the necessary citation fields.
6. When you have entered all pertinent information, click the **Insert** (fig. 4.5f) button. This will generate a wikitext citation (fig. 4.5g) that should

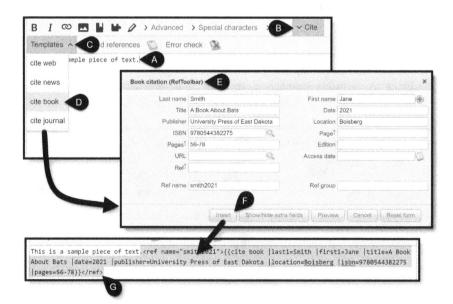

Figure 4.5. How to Work with Citation Templates

look something like this: `<ref>{{cite book |last1=Smith |first1=Jane |title=A Book About Bats |date=2021 | publisher=University Press of East Dakota |location= Boisberg |isbn=9780544382275 |pages=56-78}}</ref>` (Note that the content of these citation templates can be edited by hand, but you need to be careful that your editing does not disrupt the template's syntax.)

7. As before, make sure that the reference template `{{Reflist}}` is included on the page. If it is not, add it to the end of the article.

8. Add an **Edit summary** if necessary and click **Submit changes** to update the article with its new citation.

REPEATING A CITATION

To repeat a single citation without generating more than one entry in the article's reference section, you first need to create a named citation. To do this:

1. Navigate to an article and click **Edit source**. In the editor, place your cursor where you want to generate a citation.

2. From the editor options, click on the tab that says **Cite** and hover over **Templates**. From here, choose the type of citation template you want to use.

3. This will open the RefToolbar window. Fill in the necessary fields. Importantly, in the field labeled **Ref name**, enter a shorthand name for the citation you are creating. I recommend a combination of author's last name

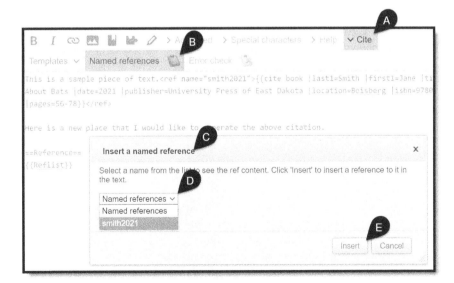

Figure 4.6. How to Reuse Citations

and the year the citation was published (e.g., `smith2021`). Once you have filled out all the necessary fields, including the Ref name slot, click **Insert**.

4. Add an **Edit summary** if necessary and click **Submit changes** to update the article with its new citation.

Now that you have generated a named citation, you can invoke it multiple times in the article without having to repeatedly create a new citation. To do this:

1. In the edit window, place your cursor where you want to repeat a citation.
2. From the editor toolbar, click on the tab that says **Cite** (fig. 4.6a).
3. Click on the checklist icon next to the words **Named references** (fig. 4.6b), which will open a window titled **Insert a named reference** (fig. 4.6c).
4. From the drop-down box labeled **Named references** (fig. 4.6d), choose the **Ref name** of the citation that you want to repeat (e.g., `smith2021`) and click **Insert** (fig. 4.6e).
5. This will insert a repeat of the initial citation. Add an **Edit summary** if necessary and click **Submit changes** to update the article.
6. After updating the page, you should now see only a single entry in the references section for the citation that you have repeatedly cited. Note, however, that small, hyperlinked letters now appear after the reference number (e.g., 1. ^ $^{a\,b\,c}$ Citation). Clicking on these letters will take you to the specific spots in the text where this one reference has been cited multiple times.

Like all things on Wikipedia, you can repeat a citation by hand, too. To do this:

1. In the edit window, place your cursor where you want to generate a citation.
2. Click on **Cite** and hover over **Templates**; choose the citational template that you want to use.
3. In the RefToolbar window, fill in the necessary fields for your citation. In the field **Ref name**, enter a shorthand name for the citation. When you are finished, click **Insert**.
4. In the editor, you should now see a wikitext citation where you placed your cursor. At the start of this citation, a string will read something like: `<ref name="...">` (e.g., `<ref name="smith2021">`). Copy this string.
5. Place your cursor where you want to repeat your citation and paste the string.
6. Within the string, place your cursor after the final quotation mark (") but before the greater-than sign (>), then add a forward slash mark: /. The wikitext should now read something like `<ref name="smith2021"/>`.
7. Pasting this exact markup string (complete with the added / mark) elsewhere in the text will generate a repeat of the initial citation.

8. When you are finished, add an **Edit summary** if necessary and click **Submit changes** to update the article.

Adding Section Headings

To add section headings into an article:

1. In the edit window, place your cursor on a blank line. (Ideally, the lines before and after should also be blank.)
2. Type the title of the heading in sentence case style (e.g., "`Like this`," "`Not Like This`").
3. Surround the text of the heading with the appropriate number of equals signs on both sides. If this is the first level in the article, start with a second-level heading (the article title itself is considered the first-level heading).
   a. To do this, add two equals signs around the title, `==Like this==`.
   b. Additional levels can be inserted simply by adding more equals signs onto both sides of a subtitle:
      i. A third level requires three equals signs around the title, `===Like this===`.
      ii. A fourth level requires four, `====Like this====`.
      iii. A fifth level requires five, `=====Like this=====`.
      iv. A sixth level requires six, `======Like this======`; note that this is the lowest heading level you can use.
4. When you are finished editing headings, add an **Edit summary** and click **Submit changes** to update the article.

Editing an Article's Talk Page

Once you become adept at working with wikitext, you will possess all the tools needed to edit article and editor talk pages. At the start of chapter 3, I discussed how each editor has their own talk page through which they can communicate with other editors. As it so happens, articles have their own talk pages, too. (Thankfully, article and editor talk pages function in the exact same way, so if you learn how to work with one type, you'll know how to work with the other.) Talk pages in general are useful because they provide space for editors to discuss the content of an article, and they can serve as a digital spot to coordinate with other editors. Unfortunately, the Visual Editor does not work on talk pages, so you will need to use wikitext if you wish to contribute to discussions.

To access an article's talk page, simply go to the top of an article, and in the upper left-hand corner of the screen, click the **Talk** tab. This will redirect you to the appropriate talk page. The first thing you likely will see is a series of boxes that tell you whether the article has been assigned to a certain WikiProject, or whether it has been peer-reviewed. After these boxes, you will then see what looks like article headings; these are individual discussion sections. To start a new discussion section:

1. Go to the top of the talk page and click the tab that says **New Section**. This will open the site's wikitext editor.
2. In the **Subject** box, type a title for your new discussion section.
3. In the big white box that takes up most of the screen, place your cursor and begin typing your message.
4. After composing your message, sign it by typing two minus signs followed immediately by four tildes: --~~~~. (Remember, when you save, Wikipedia will automatically convert this to your digital signature.)
5. When you are ready to post the message, scroll to the bottom of the edit window and click **Publish changes**. After hitting this button, your message will appear at the very bottom of the article's talk page.

Sometimes when you visit a talk page, you might want to reply to a message someone else has left. To do this:

1. Go to the talk page and find the section where you want to comment.
2. Click the **Edit source** button next to this section's heading.
3. This will open the wikitext editor. In the window, place your cursor on the line below the preceding comment and type your reply. To make discussions easier to read, editors often add a colon (:) before their comment. This tells the site to indent the comment when rendering the page:

```
This is an initial comment.-- [[User:Big_
Eptesicus|Big_Eptesicus]] ([[User talk:Big_
Eptesicus|talk]]) 9:40, 10 December 2021 (UTC)

:This is a reply to the initial comment. When
replying, use a single colon as an indentation
marker. (Be sure to also sign your comments by
typing two dashes and four tildes!)--~~~~
```

The colon thus functions like your keyboard's tab key. As such, the more colons you add to the start of your comment, the larger the indent will be:

```
This is an initial comment.-- [[User:Big_
Eptesicus|Big_Eptesicus]] ([[User talk:Big_
Eptesicus|talk]]) 9:40, 10 December 2021 (UTC)

:This is a reply to the initial comment. Note the
preceding colon.--[[User:Lil Myotis|Lil Myotis]]
([[User talk:Lil Myotis|talk]]) 9:53, 10 December
2021 (UTC)
```

```
::This is a reply to the reply (hence, two
colons).-- [[User:ButterscotchBat|ButterscotchBat]]
([[User talk:ButterscotchBat|talk]]) 10:12, 10
December 2021 (UTC)

:::This is a reply to the reply to the reply (hence,
three colons).--[[ User:Pipistrelle|Pipistrelle]]
([[User talk:Pipistrelle|talk]]) 10:22, 10 December
2021 (UTC)
```

4. When you are finished, click the **Publish changes** button. This will update the talk page to display your reply.

An Abbreviated Look at Templates

As was discussed in chapter 3, templates are among Wikipedia's most commonly used and confusing components. Unfortunately, because no two templates are alike, it would take page upon page to explain in detail the way they all work on the level of wikitext. Because of this limitation, I will focus instead in this section on how to insert a template into an article using the wikitext editor:

1. Navigate to an article and click **Edit source**. In the wikitext editor, place your cursor where you want a template.
2. From the toolbar, click the **Insert a Template** button (📽).
3. This will open the "Insert a template" pop-up window. Place your cursor in the box labeled **Search for a template** and type the name of the template you want to work with.

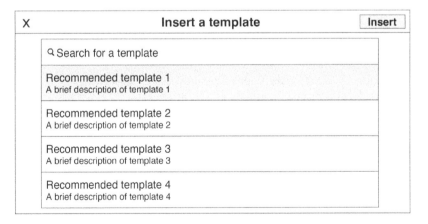

As you type, Wikipedia will recommend possible templates in a drop-down menu. When you see the template you want, select it from the menu.

4. The "Insert a template" window will then update, and on the left-hand side of the window, the template's various parameters (or "fields") are listed. Some of these must be selected; others are optional.

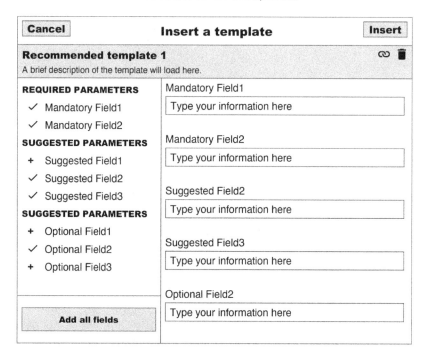

5. Activate a field by selecting it. The cross (**+**) next to the field will then turn into a checkmark (✓).
6. Fill out the forms as necessary.
7. When you are finished filling out the fields, click the **Insert** button. This will take you back to the wikitext editor screen.
8. Add an **Edit summary** if necessary and click **Submit changes** to update the article with its new template.

When examined in the wikitext editor, a template's code usually looks something like this `{{TemplateName | field1=x | field2=y | field3=etc.}}`. You can directly edit this code if you want to (e.g., you could change `field1=x` to `field1=Knuckles the Echidna`), but be careful that you don't break the code's syntax. To prevent this, ensure that you have spelled each field correctly and separated one from another by a vertical bar (|).[1] Also check that the entire template is properly named and surrounded by a closed set of double brackets (e.g., `{{, }}`).

For a detailed walk-through of how templates work, visit the Wikipedia page Help:Template (for complex template questions, visit the Wikimedia page m:Help:Advanced templates). In addition, if you are looking for the right template but you don't know what it's called, look at the Wikipedia page Wikipedia:Template index, which helpfully indexes all the templates in use on the site, ordering them by type.

A Wikitext Cheat Sheet

For many, the most complicated aspect of Wikipedia is mastering the wikitext used to, very literally, construct the site. As a way to both simplify things and summarize much of what I have covered in this chapter, I have included the following table (4.4), which functions as a "cheat sheet" outlining the basics of wikitext markup:

Table 4.4. A Wikipedia "Cheat Sheet"

Wikipedia edit	Wikitext View	Published View
Make text italic	`''Italicized Text''`	*Italicized Text*
Make text bold	`'''Bold Text'''`	**Bold Text**
Make text bold and italic	`'''''Bold and Italicized Text'''''`	***Bold and Italicized Text***
Link to another page	`[[Article name]]`	Article name
Add a piped link	`[[Article name|Different text]]`	Different text (which leads a reader to Article name)
Add an external link	`[http://www.example.org]`	[1] ⬈
	`[http://www.example.org Hyperlink with Text]`	Hyperlink with Text ⬈
Create headings	`==Section heading==` `===Subheading===` `====Further subheading====`	**Section heading** **Subheading** **Further subheading**
Add citation	`Body text of an article.<ref>Text of citation.</ref>`	Body text of an article.[1] 1. ^ Text of citation.
Add a reference section/list	`==References==` `{{Reflist}}`	**References** 1. ^ Citations will render here.

If you find wikitext really hard to parse, or you find yourself constantly "breaking" (i.e., incorrectly entering) lines of code, consider turning on **Syntax highlighting**, which can be activated through the wikitext editor by clicking on the ✏ button (fig. 4.1g). This feature illustrates through font color and emphasis how the wikitext in the editor before you is (or isn't) working. This means that if you accidentally forget to add a closing]] or }} somewhere in the text, the syntax highlighter will let you know. This tool can catch errors, big and small alike, making it an invaluable feature not only for those who are learning wikitext, but also seasoned veterans who simply want to avoid minor errors.[2]

ASSESSING QUALITY

Creating content is, of course, a major part of being a Wikipedia editor, but an equally—if not more—important part of the job is assessing the quality of articles and ensuring that they are up to code, so to speak. One way editors do this is by looking over articles and then sorting them into special categories, called "classes." An article's class functions like a letter grade, allowing editors to see quickly whether an article needs to be improved, or whether it is among the site's best. The major article classes are as follows:

- **Stub**—This is the lowest class of article. These are short pages (usually under five hundred words), and they only cover the very basics of a topic.
- **Start**—These articles are usually a bit more comprehensive than stubs, but they are still incomplete in major ways.
- **C-Class**—These articles are "substantial" and "useful to a casual reader,"[3] but they tend to have clunky prose, referencing problems, or issues with uneven coverage.
- **B-Class**—These articles are "mostly complete and without major problems."[4] They just need a bit of polish to really shine.
- **Good articles**—These are quality articles that have been assessed by an uninvolved editor.
- **Featured articles**—These are Wikipedia's best articles. Featured articles are assessed by a panel of editors.

To determine the class of an article, go to an article's **Talk** page. Usually, a few WikiProject boxes at the top of a talk page will clearly state an article's class. An article's class is also listed in the "Categories" box at the bottom of a talk page.

Peer Review

A hallmark of traditional academia is a process known as peer review, whereby a would-be scholarly publication is scrutinized by a group of (usually anonymous) experts to prevent the release of incorrect or poorly designed studies.

Believe it or not, Wikipedia has a very similar process of peer review, whereby one or more editors read an article and suggest ways that it can be improved. Although Wikipedia's reviewing process is not "blind" like academia's, nor is the process performed on every article, it still functions as a quality safeguard, helping to greatly improve an article's coverage, its readability, and its accuracy. To request that an article be peer-reviewed:

1. Go to the talk page of the article you want to have peer-reviewed and click the **Edit** tab. In the wikitext edit screen, place your cursor at the beginning of the first line and type `{{subst:PR}}` (fig. 4.7a).
2. Publish the page. You will now see a peer review box at the top of the talk page (fig. 4.7b). From this box, choose an appropriate topic for the article in question (fig. 4.7c). (If I were opening a peer review for the article Vampire bat, for instance, I would click **Natural sciences and mathematics**.)

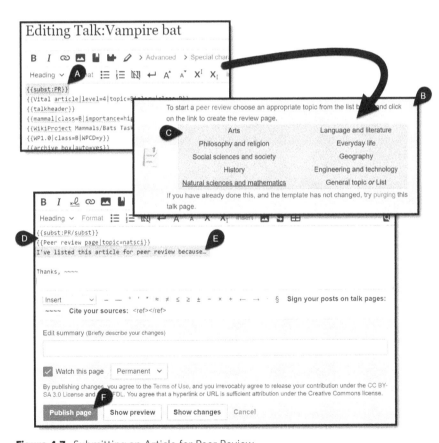

Figure 4.7. Submitting an Article for Peer Review

3. This will take you to the edit screen for the article's peer review page (fig. 4.7d). In the wikitext editor, modify or extend the text reading "I've listed this article for peer review because . . ." (fig. 4.7e), adding a rationale for why you want the article peer-reviewed.

4. When you have explained your rationale for listing the article, click the **Publish page** button (fig. 4.7f). The peer review page is now live. You can directly access this page by searching Wikipedia:Peer review/*Article Name*/archive#, replacing *Article Name* with the title of the article in question, and # with the number of times the page has been peer-reviewed (e.g., Wikipedia:Peer review/Vampire bat/archive1).

5. This page will soon be crosslisted on the Wikipedia:Peer review/List of unanswered reviews list. Now all you need to do is wait for an interested editor to add comments.

You are allowed to have only one peer review request open at a time, which means that if I were to submit Vampire bat for peer review, I could not submit Big brown bat for review until the former is closed.

Once you have gotten a knack for editing and the technicalities of Wikipedia's manual of style, you might decide to peer-review submitted articles. To do this:

1. Go to Wikipedia:Peer review/List of unanswered reviews and, from the list, find an article that you are interested in commenting on.

2. Click on the wikilink header for the article you are interested in (fig. 4.8a). (Note, this is different from the **Article**, **Article talk**, and **Watch** wikilinks *below* the header.)

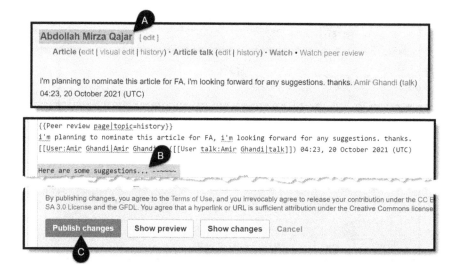

Figure 4.8. Peer-Reviewing an Article

3. This will bring you to the peer review page for the article in question (e.g., Wikipedia:Peer review/*Article Name*/archive#). Click on the **Edit** tab and, in the wikitext edit screen, add your comments below those left by the nominator (fig. 4.8b). Make sure to sign your comments by typing --~~~~.
4. When you are finished, click **Publish changes** (fig. 4.8c).
5. At this point, it is not a bad idea to reach out to the editor who submitted the article for review, informing them that you have left comments.

When you believe the peer review has run its course (due either to the nominator sufficiently responding to your comments, or because your comments have gone ignored for more than a week), you can close the review. To do this:

1. Go to the talk page of the article in question and click **Edit source**.
2. In the wikitext edit screen, remove the line reading `{{Peer review}}`. Replace it with `{{subst:Close peer review|archive=#}}`, with # once again indicating the number of times the page has been peer-reviewed.
3. Save the edit made to the talk page and then go to the peer review page (which, again, is accessible by searching `Wikipedia:Peer review/` `Article Name`/archive#).
4. Once on the peer review page, click **Edit**.
5. In the wikitext edit screen, delete the line `{{Peer review page|topic=subtopic}}` and replace it with `{{Closed peer review page}}`.

Good Articles

If you have put a lot of time and energy into improving an article, you might consider submitting it for "good article" assessment. A "good article" is the official name for a class of articles that have been judged to satisfy a set of editorial requirements. Broadly speaking, good articles are well-written, accurate, and properly cited. Visually, a "good article" can be distinguished from its less polished brethren by the presence of a small green disc (that looks like this ⊕) in its upper right-hand corner. According to Wikipedia, an article can only be deemed "good" if it is:

1. **Well-Written**—First, the article should be well-written, its structure should comply with Wikipedia's manual of style, and its language should be understandable to a general audience. This latter point can be tricky if the subject of the article is complex or technical. To ensure that an article is understandable to a broad audience, use common language as much as possible, avoid heavy use of jargon, spell out acronyms when they are introduced, and provide examples when describing abstract concepts.[5]

2. **Verifiable and Devoid of Original Research**—A good article is citational, reflecting only what published sources have to say about the topic. Every assertion must be backed up with a citation, and any assertion for which a source cannot be provided (i.e., "original research") must be culled. (For more on these topics, see the subsections of chapter 2 titled "Wikipedia Is Citational" and "Wikipedia Is Never Original.")

3. **Broad in Its Coverage**—A good article should provide a broad overview of its subject matter, balancing a somewhat abstract "bigger picture" understanding with a detailed look at the topic. In other words, an article should neither be so general that it only superficially explores a topic, nor so granular that the average reader will find themselves in the weeds after only a few sentences. (A general rule of thumb is that an article should summarize a topic—not regurgitate every single fact about it.)

4. **Neutral**—A good article should be written in a way that presents all major viewpoints fairly, and the article should showcase these viewpoints relative to their appearance in the existing literature. Articles also should not be promotional or give too much attention to fringe theories. (For more on this topic, see the subsection of chapter 2 titled "Wikipedia's Content Is Neutral.")

5. **Stable**—The penultimate element to consider is whether the article is stable. Stability is important, because although articles change over time, they first need to demonstrate a sort of consistent excellence before they can be judged as "good."

6. **Illustrated (If Possible)**—Finally, the article should, if at all possible, be illustrated or accentuated with some sort of media. The Wikimedia Commons hosts millions of freely licensed images, video, and audio files that an editor can add to a good article nominee. Not only does this sort of media enliven an article, but it can also help (literally) illustrate the finer details of a more complex topic. Images and the like should be captioned and, ideally, have alt-text. Finally, any non-free media must comply with fair use guidelines and satisfy Wikipedia's criteria for inclusion.

In a nutshell, the good article review process is akin to the scholarly peer review process, only both the nominator and the reviewer are known to one another (i.e., it is not "blind"). To submit an article for good article review, an editor should follow these steps:

1. First, improve an article so that it fulfills the six good article criteria. (Attention should be placed on polishing the article's prose and meticulously sourcing all claims.)
2. Then, go to the talk page of the article and click the **Edit source** tab. In the wikitext editor, place your cursor on the first line and paste `{{subst:GAN|subtopic=Subtopic Name}}`; replace `Subtopic Name` with one of the thirty valid subtopic labels found at Wikipedia:GAN/I#N2 (fig. 4.9a).

Figure 4.9. Nominating a Potential "Good Article"

3. Click **Publish changes**. You will now see a good article nomination box at the top of the talk page (fig. 4.9b).
4. A bot will soon crosslist the article on the Wikipedia:Good article nominations page. Now all you must do is wait for an interested editor to come along and review the article.
5. When a reviewer agrees to look over the article, they will create a review page for it, located at Talk:*Article Name*/GA#, with *Article Name* being the name of a page, and # being the number of times the article has been reviewed (e.g., Talk:Little brown bat/GA1).
6. On this page, the reviewer can **pass** the article, **fail** it, or put it **on hold** for additional edits to be made. If the reviewer requests changes, the nominator should do their best to modify the article until the reviewer is satisfied. If an article is failed, the nominator can refine the article and resubmit it when they feel it is ready.

If you are interested in reviewing an article, the steps are as follows:

1. First, familiarize yourself with the good article criteria discussed at the start of this section. This will help you zone in on areas of an article that might need attention.

2. Next, go to the <u>Wikipedia:Good article nominations</u> page (fig. 4.10a) and find an article that you want to review (fig. 4.10b). Click on **start review** link next to that article's name (fig. 4.10c).
3. This will redirect you to the wikitext editor, through which you can create a review page for the article. All you need to do at this stage is click **Publish page**.
4. This will create the good article review page, titled <u>Talk:*Article Name*/GA#</u> (with *Article Name* being the name of a page, and # being the number of times the article has been reviewed; fig. 4.10d).
5. Now, read the article and make note of any issues that you see.

Figure 4.10. Reviewing a "Good Article" Candidate

6. When you are ready to list those issues, go back to the good article review page (again, located at <u>Talk:*Article Name*/GA#</u>) and click the **Edit** (fig. 4.10e) button next to the "GA Review" header.
7. Use the wikitext editor to list any issues you see with the article. Some editors like to structure their review around the six good article criteria; others prefer to read the article and make comments as they come across issues. Either approach is acceptable. To save, click **Publish Changes** at the bottom of the edit window.

Once you finish your analysis of the article, you have the power to pass the article, fail it, or put it on hold. To **pass** an article:

1. Go to that article's talk page and click the **Edit source** tab.
2. In the edit screen, replace the line `{{GA nominee|...|status=onreview}}` with `{{GA|~~~~~|topic=|page=}}`.
3. In the `topic=` field, provide an appropriate keyword from the <u>Wikipedia:WikiProject Good articles/Topic Values</u> page.
4. In the `page=` field, type the review number (e.g., the # value mentioned earlier).
5. Click **Publish changes**. A bot will add the good article icon and let the nominator know that their submission passed.

Conversely, if a reviewer decides to **fail** an article, they should:

1. Go to that article's talk page and click the **Edit source** tab.
2. In the edit screen, replace the line `{{GA nominee|...|status=onreview}}` with `{{FailedGA|~~~~~|topic=|page=}}`.
3. In the `topic=` field, provide an appropriate keyword from the <u>Wikipedia:WikiProject Good articles/Topic Values</u> page.
4. In the `page=` field, type the review number (e.g., the # value mentioned earlier).
5. Click **Publish changes**. A bot will let the nominator know that their submission failed.

Finally, if the reviewer wants to put the article **on hold** so that the nominator can make additional changes, they should:

1. Go to that article's talk page and click the **Edit source** tab.
2. Locate the `{{GA nominee|...|status=onreview}}` line.
3. Change the `status=` field to `onhold`.
4. Click **Publish changes**. A bot will let the nominator know that their submission is temporarily in limbo.

5. Once a reviewer is ready to pass or fail the article, they can follow the steps previously outlined.

When an article passes the good article review process, a bot will automatically add the article to Wikipedia:Good articles; the bot will then add the green shield icon in the upper right-hand corner of the article itself, which lets readers know that the article is officially "good."

Featured Articles

Sometimes, after you have spent months (if not years) editing and reediting an article, you might think to yourself, *Wow! Not to toot my own horn, but this page is excellent*. If your article passed its good article review with flying colors and has only blossomed in quality since then, consider submitting that article for "featured article" assessment. Featured articles are widely regarded as the site's best and most rigorously sourced articles, and many editors liken them to "professional" encyclopedia articles such as the ones published in the *Encyclopaedia Britannica*, and so forth. As of December 2021, 6,048 articles out of 6.42 million have earned "featured" status, meaning they represent only a hair over 0.09 percent of all Wikipedia's articles. Similar to good articles, featured articles are distinguished from others by the presence of a small gold star (that looks like this ★) in their upper right-hand corner.

To earn "featured" status, an article must meet four key requirements, which stipulate that a feature article:

1. **Has Content of the Highest Quality**—A featured article should be thoroughly researched, making use of the highest quality sources available. In terms of prose, a featured article should be clear, engaging, and free from typos or other readability issues. The article should also be neutral, stable, and logically organized.

2. **Follows the Wikipedia Manual of Style**—A featured article must comply exactly with the many rules explicated in Wikipedia's Manual of Style. In particular, the article must have a concise lead section that summarizes the article's contents, it must be laid out appropriately, and its citations need to be consistently formatted.

3. **Is Illustrated, If Possible**—Like a good article, a featured article should be illustrated with pertinent media files, such as images, video snippets, or sound bites. (Although media is technically not required, it is assumed that a featured article will have at least some form of illustration.) Media integrated into the article must be captioned and have alt-text, where appropriate. Finally, any non-free media must comply with fair use guidelines and satisfy Wikipedia's criteria for inclusion.

4. **Is of an Appropriate Article Length**—If good articles must be "broad" in coverage, then featured articles must be comprehensive, summarizing every

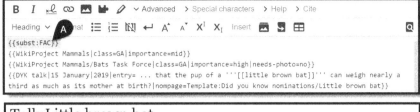

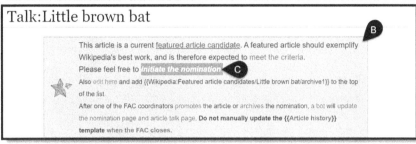

Figure 4.11. Nominating a Potential "Featured Article" (Part 1)

major aspect of a topic in appropriate detail. Nothing major should be left out of the article, but undo weight should still not be given to minor details.

To earn the featured article label, an article must be reviewed by not just one but a group of Wikipedia editors. These reviewers must reach a consensus, which is determined by an impartial featured article coordinator. As with good article review, the featured article nomination process mirrors an open form of academic peer review. To nominate a page for featured article consideration:

1. Prep the article according to Wikipedia's Manual of Style, ensure that the article's prose is of the highest quality, and check that its references are properly formatted. It is also a good idea to request that the article be peer-reviewed before you submit it for featured article consideration (but make sure that the peer review is closed before you begin the featured article nomination); I also recommend that you reach out to an editor skilled in copyediting and request that they look at the article.

2. When you believe the page is ready, go to its talk page and click the **Edit source** tab. In the wikitext edit screen, place your cursor on the first line and paste `{{subst:FAC}}` (fig. 4.11a).
3. Click **Publish changes**. You will now see a featured article nomination box at the top of the talk page (fig. 4.11b).
4. Click the redlink that reads **initiate the nomination** (fig. 4.11c). This will bring you to a new edit screen with preloaded content. Replace the text reading `This article is about...` (fig. 4.11d) with your rationale for nominating the article.
5. When you are finished, click **Publish page**. This creates a review page for the article in question.
6. Next, go to <u>Wikipedia:Featured article candidates</u> and scroll to the section titled "Nominations" (fig. 4.12e). Click the **edit** button next to this section heading (fig. 4.12f).
7. In the edit window, paste `{{Wikipedia:Featured article candidates/`*`Article Name`*`/archive#}}` on the first line after the heading itself; replace *Article Name* with the title of page you are nominating, and replace # with the number of times the article has been nominated for featured status (e.g., `{{Wikipedia:Featured article candidates/Little brown bat/archive1}}`) (fig. 4.12g).

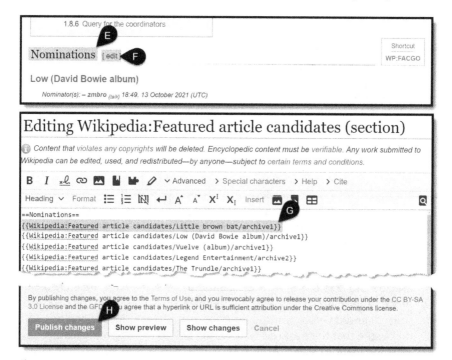

Figure 4.12. Nominating a Potential "Featured Article" (Part 2)

8. Click **Publish changes** (fig. 4.12h).
9. Wait for editors to leave comments. If these editors make suggestions, respond to them accordingly.

If you want to support, oppose, or comment on another editor's featured article nomination, follow these steps:

1. Go to Wikipedia:Featured article candidates#Nominations (fig. 4.13a) and scroll down until you see a nomination to which you wish to contribute (fig. 4.13b). Click on the **Edit** link next to the article title (fig. 4.13c).
2. This will open the wikitext edit screen. From here, you have several options:
   a. If you support the nomination, go to a new line at the bottom of the edit screen and type * '''Support''' (fig. 4.13d). List the reasons why you think the article deserves to be elevated to featured status, then sign your username.
   b. If you oppose the nomination, go to a new line at the bottom of the edit screen and type * '''Oppose''' (fig. 4.13e). Then list the reasons why you think the article does not deserve to be featured before signing your username.
   c. If you just want to leave comments without voicing support or opposition, go to a new line at the bottom of the edit screen and type

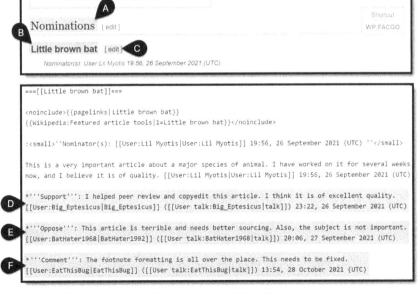

Figure 4.13. Commenting on a "Featured Article" Candidate

* `'''Comment'''` (fig. 4.13f), followed by your comments and your username.

3. When you are finished, click **Publish changes**. It is often a good idea to then reach out to the editor who nominated the article via their talk page to let them know you commented.

Eventually, consensus will be reached. If an article fails to be promoted, the nominator must wait two weeks before resubmitting (and in the interim, use any lessons learned during the failed nomination to improve the article). If the article passes, a bot will automatically add it to Wikipedia:Featured articles; the bot will also insert in the upper right-hand corner of the article the small star icon, denoting to all that the article is "featured" content.

Protecting Articles

Sometimes, articles for whatever reason function as vandal magnets, attracting wave after wave of unconstructive edits. If one of these pages is on your Watchlist, reverting all the vandalism can get quite tiring. Luckily, a mechanism exists by which an article can be locked, allowing only certain editors to modify the page; this mechanism is referred to as article "protection." You can tell whether an article has been protected by looking in the upper right-hand corner of the page (where the "good" and "featured" article icons are located): If you see a small lock icon (🔒), that means that the page has been protected from certain editors. Various levels of protection exist, but those you are most likely to encounter are full protection, semi-protection, extended confirmed protection, and pending changes protection. The first of these, full, means that only administrators can edit the protected article. This level is usually reserved for heavily trafficked templates or elements of the MediaWiki namespace. However, it can also be invoked as a sort of "nuclear option" to end an edit war. By locking an article to all, full protection forces all sides in an edit war to negotiate the problem on the article's talk page.[6]

One level down from full protection is semi-protection, which blocks anonymous editors from making changes to an article. This is a common setting, given that it bars anonymous IP editors—a group disproportionately responsible for most acts of vandalism—from disrupting what usually are quite popular pages. If vandalism turns out to be caused by not only IPs, but also newly created accounts, an admin can increase the efficacy of semi-protection by switching to extended confirmed protection. This prohibits IPs as well as auto-confirmed editors (i.e., users who have had their account for less than thirty days and have made fewer than five hundred edits) from modifying an article. The final level of article protection is pending changes protection. Under this system, unregistered users and newly created accounts can submit suggested edits to a page, but these edits must be approved by an editor who has "pending changes reviewer" rights. The benefit here is that anonymous editors can suggest changes, but registered users still have the power to catch unproductive edits.

If an article you created or are watching has started to experience heavy vandalism, you can always reach out to an admin to request page protection. To do this:

1. Go to Wikipedia:Requests for page protection.
2. In the blue box titled "Requests for page protection," click **Request protection**.
3. This will redirect you to a new screen. Enter the title of the article in question and then provide, in detail, why the article needs protection. When you are finished, click **Submit request**.
4. An admin will review your request and determine whether protection is needed. If they agree with your concerns, protection will be provided; if they reject your request, nothing happens.

Sometimes, an article can be given a level of protection that is too strong, stifling its growth. If you believe an article needs to have its protection level downgraded, you can likewise submit this request to an admin. To do this:

1. Go to Wikipedia:Requests for page protection.
2. In the blue box titled "Requests for page protection," click **Request unprotection**.
3. This will redirect you to a new screen. Enter the title of the article in question and then provide, in detail, why the article needs to have its protection downgraded or removed. When you are finished, click **Submit request**.
4. An admin will review your request, and if they agree with you, they will remove or downgrade the article's protection.

Deleting Articles

One of Wikipedia's better-known (or perhaps "infamous") processes is the method by which articles are deleted from the site. Pages are to be deleted only if they do not fit the scope of the site, or if there are fundamental issues with the article's content (e.g., plagiarism, copyright violation). There are several ways to begin the deletion process. The quickest method, called "speedy deletion," is used only when an article is "so obviously inappropriate for Wikipedia that [it would] have no chance of surviving a [full-on] deletion discussion."[7] Factors that make an article a likely candidate for speedy deletion include "patent nonsense," extensive vandalism, hoax pages, promotional articles, and articles that make threats, among many others (for a full list, see the article Wikipedia:Criteria for speedy deletion). To nominate an article for speedy deletion:

1. Go to the article and edit it using the wikitext editor.
2. Add the wikicode `{{db|Reason}}` to the top of the article; replace *Reason* with a succinct argument for why the article should be speedily deleted.
3. Click **Publish changes**.

This tag will soon draw the attention of an admin. They will then look at the page and, if they feel that it deserves to be excised, they will delete the article. If someone has nominated an article for speedy deletion that you otherwise believe should be retained, you can click on the **Contest this speedy deletion** link located in the deletion tag at the top of the article. This will take you to a discussion page, where you can express your opinions as to why the article should remain live.

For an article that you feel should be removed from the site but does not satisfy the criteria for speedy deletion, you can always propose the article for standard deletion. To do this:

1. Go to the article and edit it using the wikitext editor.
2. Add the wikicode `{{subst:prod|Reason}}` to the top of the article; replace *Reason* with your argument for why you think the article should be removed.
3. Click **Publish changes**.

This will add a tag at the start of the article, indicating that it has been nominated for deletion. If seven days pass and no one has objected to the notice, an admin will delete the article. The big difference between the speedy deletion and standard deletion processes is time; the former is, as its name suggests, a speedy process, whereas the latter is a much slower process reserved for matters that are not urgent.

Sometimes you might find an article that you believe is so obviously out of place, but when you go to delete it, you are surprised to find that a gaggle of editors have popped out from behind the metaphorical bushes, vehemently opposing your proposed deletion. In instances such as this, it is usually a good idea to start a discussion with the wider community at Wikipedia:Articles for deletion. Also referred to as "AfD," this page is a portal dedicated to discussions about deletion proposals. To start a new discussion:

1. Go to the subsection of Wikipedia:Articles for deletion titled "Creating an AfD"[8] (fig. 4.14a).
2. In the search box, type `Wikipedia:Articles for deletion/ Title`, replacing *Title* with the name of the article you are discussing (fig. 4.14b).

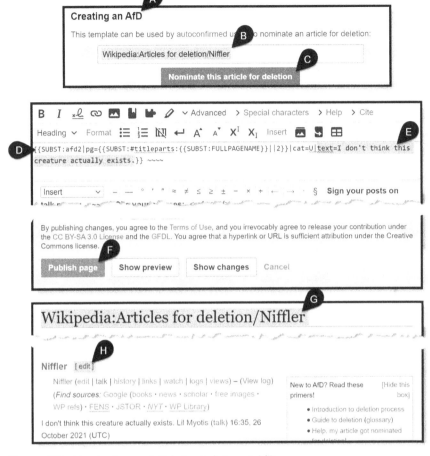

Figure 4.14. Nominating an Article for Deletion at AfD

3. Click the **Nominate this article for deletion** link (fig. 4.14c). This will redirect you to the wikitext editor.

4. In the editor screen, you will see a line of already generated wikitext (fig. 4.14d). In this string of letters and symbols, locate the text reading `text=Reason` and replace `Reason` with your argument for why the article should be deleted (fig. 4.14e).

5. Click **Publish page** (fig. 4.14f). This will create a new discussion page (located at Wikipedia:Articles for deletion/*Title*, with the name of the article in place of "*Title*," e.g., Wikipedia:Articles for deletion/Niffler; fig. 4.14g). Other editors can voice their support for or opposition to your request by going to this page, clicking **Edit** (fig. 4.14h), and stating their case.

A discussion about deleting an article is not a simple vote; instead, it is a procedure that seeks consensus, all of which is grounded in the site's established guidelines. If you wish to chime in on such a discussion:

1. Either go to the article's deletion discussion directly (e.g., Wikipedia:Articles for deletion/*Title*), or search for that discussion at Wikipedia:Articles for deletion. Once you have found the discussion, click **Edit source**; this will open the wikitext edit screen.
2. On the bottom line of the page, place your cursor underneath any other comments and type * followed by a brief and emboldened summary of your stance (e.g., if you support the article's deletion, type * `'''Delete'''`, if you disagree, type * `'''Keep'''`, etc.). You can then expand on your reasoning before signing off with your signature (i.e., `--~~~~`).
3. When you are finished, click **Publish changes**.

In the wikitext editor, an article deletion discussion will look something like this:

```
I don't think this creature actually exists. [[User:Lil
Myotis|Lil Myotis]] ([[User talk:Lil Myotis|talk]])
16:35, 26 October 2021 (UTC)

* '''Comment''': I believe I saw one steal a penny
once.-- [[User:ButterscotchBat|ButterscotchBat]] ([[User
talk:ButterscotchBat|talk]]) 19:43, 26 October 2021
(UTC)

* '''Delete''': This is a fictional animal.--
[[User:Big_Eptesicus|Big_Eptesicus]] ([[User talk:Big_
Eptesicus|talk]]) 9:22, 27 October 2021 (UTC)

* '''Keep''': This is a real animal. I only
know that because I'm allergic to them.--
[[ User:Pipistrelle|Pipistrelle]] ([[User
talk:Pipistrelle|talk]]) 5:07, 29 October 2021 (UTC)
```

After seven days, an admin who was not involved with the discussion will review the points made and either approve the deletion request or deny it. At this point, consensus is not always clear, so sometimes an admin will close an AfD by recording that "no consensus" was reached; this means that the article will not be deleted at that moment, but it could be removed in the future if another discussion raises better arguments.

Often, deletion of an article is an unnecessary exercise in bureaucracy. This is especially true when one article can be quietly and (usually) noncontroversially redirected to another article. On Wikipedia, the term "redirect" refers to a page that, when searched for, sends the reader automatically to a different article. For a cogent example, if I type "Niffler" into the Wikipedia search bar and hit enter, I am immediately brought to the page titled <u>Magical creatures in Harry Potter</u>; this is because, on its own, a <u>Niffler</u> article would not be very substantial, so it has been set up to automatically send readers to a broader, more comprehensive page. To redirect an article, simply replace its contents with the following bit of wikitext: #REDIRECT `Target article`, replacing "Target article" with the name of the page to which you want to send readers. Redirects can be created quickly, they are easy to undo, and they can be performed by any editor—admin privileges are not required. Before nominating an article for deletion, ask: "Can this article be quietly redirected to another page?" If the answer is yes, avoid going the AfD route.

WIKIPROJECTS AND TASK FORCES

A final way to grow as a Wikipedia editor is to collaborate with other Wikipedians, and one of the easiest ways to do this is to join a WikiProject. This unique term refers to a group dedicated to expanding and improving Wikipedia's coverage of a particular topic; for instance, members of "WikiProject History" are dedicated to improving articles about world history, whereas the editors in "WikiProject Mammals" focus their attention on mammalian articles. WikiProjects each get their own page (located in Wikipedia namespace at <u>Wikipedia:WikiProject *Project name*</u>), which serves as a central hub for the project's many editors. This page is a powerful organization tool, providing editors with an easily accessible digital space in which they can better coordinate article improvements. Because WikiProjects have a scope (i.e., a range of articles that relates directly to the group's raison d'être), it is common for members to create lists of articles that need to be improved or created. Other projects keep track of their "wins" by documenting how many good or featured articles are under the purview of their topic.

To provide a more concrete example of how WikiProjects work, consider my experience as a member of "*The X-Files* WikiProject," dedicated to improving articles related to the Fox sci-fi television series *The X-Files*. I joined this group in 2011 (then located at <u>Wikipedia:WikiProject The X-Files</u>),[9] and in time, I became one of its more active members. On the WikiProject's main page, members of the group created a list of articles that we wanted to create or update, and we showcased our best articles in a "Recognized content" section. Likewise, we used the talk page as a digital space to make suggestions and to determine which episodes we wanted to focus our energy on. Within a few short years, *The X-Files* WikiProject had created a unique page for every episode of the series; in the process, we had also churned out 265 good articles and 14 featured articles. Much of this success was due to the WikiProject's digital infrastructure, which facilitated our discussions and improvement plans, allowing us to work quickly and efficiently with one another.

Some WikiProjects are so large that they are further subdivided into smaller task forces, which focus on a specific aspect of the overall project topic. For instance, I am a member of the Bats Task Force (Wikipedia:BATS), a subgroup of the larger WikiProject Mammals. Task forces and WikiProjects are similar in many ways, and according to Wikipedia itself, the main difference between the two is "that [a] task force minimizes bureaucratic overhead," whereas a WikiProject "provide[s] much of the procedural and technical infrastructure" on which a task force is established.[10] As such, task forces tend to be more ad hoc, whereas WikiProjects are more structured. Regardless of any differences, both task forces and WikiProjects are critical mechanisms that have helped the site leverage the power of many to improve Wikipedia's coverage of topic areas.

The accomplishments of the many WikiProjects—be it the "Military history" WikiProject's promotion of 1,349 articles to featured status or the "Women in Red" WikiProject's creation of 177,984 new articles about women—are proof positive that large groups of editors, when properly organized and inspired, can do marvelous things. And although it might sound corny, I believe that the fundamental spirit of collaboration that drives WikiProjects is a wonderful typification of a camaraderie specific to the site—a "Wiki-teamwork," if you will. As of early 2022, I am happy to report that this Wiki-teamwork is still going strong—around two thousand WikiProjects are in existence, a full list of which can be found at Wikipedia:WikiProject Council/Directory (however, note that not all of these projects are currently active). To join one of these projects, all you need to do is go to the group's main page. Usually, this page will include a list of participants, onto which you are invited to edit in your username. Once on the list, you are officially part of the project and can contribute as you see best fit. Happy editing!

5

Concrete Ways to Make Wikipedia a Better Resource

When explaining to interested crowds how Wikipedia works, I always make sure to emphasize that although the site is (in my opinion) one of the greatest human creations of the past five hundred years, it still has issues. Indeed, everything from minor typos to misapplied sources can be found on the site. But before I drive away any would-be editors with needless doom and gloom, I also stress that we, as potential authors of Wikipedia, have the power to rectify those flaws through responsible editing practices. This tends to hearten the people to whom I speak, but it also tends to provoke a very specific question: "What exactly can I do to make Wikipedia better?"

In the first half of this chapter, I focus on six activities that I believe have the greatest potential to effect real change on the site; these include copyediting articles, fact-checking citations, translating articles from other language editions of Wikipedia, uploading images to Wikimedia Commons, thinking about accessibility considerations, and hosting "edit-a-thons." The chapter's second half is a more specialized discussion of how people who work at cultural institutions (such as galleries, libraries, archives, or museums, often colloquially referred to by the acronym "GLAMs"), as well as those who work in the classroom, can bring Wikipedia into their spheres of influence.

COPYEDITING

Copyediting is the art of combing through text, fixing typos, improving syntax, expanding contractions, breaking up run-on sentences, and adjusting punctuation. In *The Copyeditor's Handbook*, Amy Einsohn and Marilyn Schwartz argue that a copyeditor's main concern is with "the '4 Cs'—clarity, coherency, consistency, and correctness—in service of the 'Cardinal C': communication."[1] Copyediting is thus more than just "fixing errors" or "proofreading"; it is a process to improve a text's readability. Thus, copyeditors on Wikipedia tend to focus on making the site's text clearer and easier to understand. Because these sorts of editors focus largely on the syntax of the site's text, they need not have expert content knowledge. (That said, a copyeditor must be careful that edits do not change the meaning of a sentence, or that modifications do not misrepresent a source.) Copyediting might be a good way to volunteer if you enjoy refining others' prose, or if you hope to hone your skills as a technical writer.[2]

Editors interested in copyediting the English version of Wikipedia should look at its "Manual of Style" (commonly referred to as the "MoS").[3] This detailed guide lays out the ways that the site's content is to be written and formatted, stylistically speaking. Although this manual is too long to explicate in just a few short paragraphs, there are two rules that I believe it best for new editors to learn right away. First, when it comes to quotation, the English Wikipedia follows the rules of "logical punctuation."[4] This approach—sometimes colloquially called the "British style"[5]—simply means that when quoting a full sentence, an editor should place terminal punctuation (i.e., periods, exclamation points, or question marks) on the inside of the quotation marks only if that punctuation appeared in the original. Consider the following example:

Source: My favorite animal is the little brown bat.
Quotation: Paul Thomas once said, "My favorite animal is the little brown bat."

Because the example quotation here repeats the entirety of the source text, the terminal punctuation (i.e., the period) is inside the quotation marks. Now, consider this second example:

Source: My favorite animal is the little brown bat.
Quotation: Did Paul just say, "My favorite animal is the little brown bat"?

Because the question mark does not appear in the source text, it has been placed *outside* the quotation marks.

Similarly, when quoting a few words or a sentence fragment, place any necessary punctuation on the outside of the quotation markers:

Source: Lawrence is a wonderful city located in Eastern Kansas.
Quotation: Paul Thomas has argued that Lawrence "is a wonderful city", but this is an assertion that is not shared by all.

For those of you who were told in grade school that punctuation must always be placed on the inside of quotation marks (an approach often referred to as the "American style"),[6] the specifics of logical punctuation might initially throw you for a loop. But as with all things on Wikipedia, practice makes perfect. And remember, if you do make a mistake, you can always revert it.

The second stylistic point to remember is that although all articles on the English Wikipedia are, perhaps unsurprisingly, written in English, those about British topics are to be written using the British spelling of words (e.g., "London is a *centre* of the *Labour* Party"), whereas articles about American topics are to be written using the American spelling (e.g., "They went to the *theater* to see their *favorite* film"). Similarly, it is common that articles about British topics will use the "Day Month Year" format for dates (e.g., 1 January 2021), whereas articles about American topics will use the "Month Day, Year" format (e.g., January 1, 2021). Regarding the date style, neither approach is wrong, and editors are free to use the format that they prefer; the main thing to keep an eye out for is consistent use within a given article.

Table 5.1. Suggestions for Further Reading

Butcher, Judith, Caroline Drake, and Maureen Leach. *Butcher's Copy-Editing: The Cambridge Handbook for Editors, Copy-Editors and Proofreaders*. Cambridge, UK: Cambridge University Press, 2006.

Einsohn, Amy, and Marilyn Schwartz. *The Copyeditor's Handbook: A Guide for Book Publishing and Corporate Communications*. 4th ed. Oakland, CA: University of California Press, 2019.

New Oxford Style Manual. 3rd ed. Oxford, UK: Oxford University Press, 2016.

Tony1. "User:Tony1/How to improve your writing." Wikipedia, accessed January 25, 2022. https://en.wikipedia.org/wiki/User:Tony1/How_to_improve_your_writing

"Wikipedia:Basic copyediting." Wikipedia, accessed July 27, 2021. https://en.wikipedia.org/w/index.php?title=Wikipedia:Basic_copyediting&oldid=1032713303.

FACT-CHECKING

In the social and natural sciences, interest in reporting novel findings is so great that researchers have a disincentive to rerun and verify older experiments. This bias against replication means that a good number of "statistically significant" studies are actually false positives. An analogous problem exists on Wikipedia: many editors are excited to create new articles or write up new content for Wikipedia, but not nearly as many are as enthusiastic about going through existing articles and checking to see whether the existing content is accurate. As a result, buried in the text of Wikipedia are myriad errors. To overcome this bias, Wikipedia is in desperate need of fact-checkers, or people who seek out the sources cited in articles and ensure that they say what the article claims they do.

When I visit classrooms to talk about Wikipedia, I like to stress the importance of "Wiki-fact-checking" by telling the story of the Bicholim conflict article.[7] Created on July 4, 2007, this article described a short war between the Portuguese Empire and the Maratha Empire in the seventeenth century. The article, which comprised forty-five hundred words, was fairly well written: it featured readable prose, logical section divisions, interesting images, and copious citations. It even was reviewed by another editor and officially certified a "good article." There was one problem: the "Bicholim conflict" was fictitious, and the article had been created as a hoax! But because no one bothered to fact-check the article, no one questioned its veracity. The ruse only came to an end in 2012 when an editor named User:ShelfSkewed attempted to track down the books mentioned in the article. When User:ShelfSkewed was unable to find any of the sources, that editor brought the discovery to the community's attention, and the article was deleted after swift deliberation. Although the community eventually detected the fraud, the fact that it took editors almost five years to do so is rather alarming (not to mention embarrassing). I do not mean to appeal to fear with this anecdote; I simply believe that the Bicholim conflict hoax is the perfect cautionary tale for why editors should fact-check articles. Sometimes, misinformation on Wikipedia is easy to spot, but other times, misinformation is more insidious, disguised in the trappings of what otherwise looks like "good" content.

For those who want to fact-check but who do not know where to look for quality sources, fear not. Excellent material can often be found freely via Google Books or Google Scholar. There also exists a variety of publishers—including the Public Library of Science (perhaps best known for its journal *PLOS One*), punctum books, and the Open Humanities Press—offer rigorous research free of charge. (Caveat editor: The quality of free and open-access content can vary wildly. As such, I recommend that you consult the Directory of Open Access Journals[8] or the Open Access Directory[9] to help you find reputable publishers of open-access content.)

Wikipedia editors also have the opportunity to sign up for a "Wikipedia Library" card, which provides free digital access to dozens of reputable publishers and scholarly collections, including Cambridge University Press, the Cochrane Library, Emerald Group Publishing, MIT Press Journals, the Loeb Classical Library, and Oxford Scholarship Online (among many others). To receive a card, you must be an editor in good standing, have accumulated more than five hundred edits over six months of editing, and have made more than ten edits in the previous month.[10]

Table 5.2. Suggestions for Further Reading

Borel, Brooke. *The Chicago Guide to Fact-Checking*. Chicago: University of Chicago Press, 2016.

Hudgins, Darren, and Jennifer LaGarde. *Fact vs. Fiction: Teaching Critical Thinking Skills in the Age of Fake News*. Portland, OR: International Society for Technology in Education, 2018.

Smith, Sarah Harrison. *The Fact Checker's Bible: A Guide to Getting It Right*. New York: Anchor, 2007.

"Wikipedia:Verifiability." Wikipedia, accessed July 27, 2021. https://en.wikipedia.org/w/index.php?title=Wikipedia:Verifiability&oldid=1035296806.

TRANSLATING ARTICLES

As of January 2022, Wikipedia has 325 different language editions. Each variant almost certainly has its fair share of entries exclusive to that version of Wikipedia. If you are multilingual, one novel way to help expand Wikipedia is to scour other language editions of Wikipedia for unique articles and then translate them into English for inclusion on the English Wikipedia.[11] (The opposite is also true: editors can translate English articles into a different language for inclusion on that language's edition of Wikipedia.)[12] Be aware that Wikipedia discourages users from exclusively using machine translation tools such as Google Translate. Although these programs are useful, when presented with paragraphs of text, they tend to miss linguistic nuance. The result is often a lexical blob replete with grammatical issues, awkward sentence constructions, and the literal rendering of idioms and slang.[13] When in doubt, reach out to other editors who are familiar with the languages you are working with.

Content from any language-variant of Wikipedia can be reused for other projects without permission. That said, Wikipedia's license still requires that this reuse be attributed appropriately; this applies to translations, too. The easiest way to do this is by including with your translation edit a detailed edit summary pointing readers to the original article. Per the guidelines laid out in the article Wikipedia:Copying within Wikipedia, Wikipedia[14] recommends a variation of the following: `Content in this edit is translated from the existing` *`Specific Language`* `Wikipedia article at [[`*`Source Language Code:Name of article`*`]]; see its history for attribution.`

In that example, `Source Language Code` refers to the portion of a Wikipedia URL that identifies the language of the site in question. The English Wikipedia's language code, for instance, is "en" (hence why the site is found at *en*.wikipedia.org), whereas the German Wikipedia's code is "de" (meaning that it is found at *de*.wikipedia.org). Were I to edit the English article Great Pyramid of Giza and include translated text from the German article de:Cheops-Pyramide, my edit summary would need to look like this: `Content in this edit is translated from the existing German Wikipedia article at [[de:Cheops-Pyramide]]; see its history for attribution.` (If you forget or neglect to include this note in your edit summary, do not panic. You can always post on the article's talk page, explaining that your contributions were translated from a different version of Wikipedia.)

Table 5.3. Suggestions for Further Reading

"Content Translation." MediaWiki, accessed January 10, 2022. https://www.mediawiki
.org/wiki/Content_translation.

"Designing a Translation Assignment." Wiki Education, accessed July 27, 2021. https://
dashboard.wikiedu.org/training/instructors/designing-a-translation-assignment.

Help:Translation. Wikipedia, accessed July 27, 2021. https://en.wikipedia.org/w/index
.php?title=Help:Translation&oldid=1028152966.

McAndrew, Ewan. "Wikipedia in Curriculum for Translation Studies MSc." Wikimedia
Report, January, 2017. https://upload.wikimedia.org/wikipedia/commons/c/c3/
Wikipedia_in_the_Classroom_-_Translation_Studies_MSc_case_study.pdf.

UPLOADING IMAGES

If you are more of a visual person, you can also contribute to the site by uploading your own images to the Wikimedia Commons[15] (https://commons
.wikimedia.org/wiki/Main_Page); this will allow your images to be used freely and easily on all Wikipedia variants. But before I discuss how you upload images, it is important to talk about which images you can upload. With a few exceptions, Wikimedia Commons requires that uploads be licensed for *free and open reuse, even in commercial projects.* The easiest way to ensure that your contributions meet these requirements is by releasing them into the public domain, or under a Creative Commons license.

As was briefly discussed in chapter 2, the public domain refers to material that anyone can use without permission or the need to pay royalties, and so forth. In the United States, works usually fall into the public domain seventy years after the creator's death,[16] but sometimes, creators release their works immediately into the public domain in the spirit of openness. The catch is that doing so means relinquishing total ownership of the work. Conversely, a creator who releases work under a Creative Commons license retains the copyright but stipulates situations in which that work can be used freely by others. A variety of Creative Commons licenses are available to choose from, but when uploading images to Wikimedia Commons, one of these three is preferred:

1. **CC0**—A work released under this license is akin to releasing a work into the public domain. CC0 works can thus be used freely by anyone for any purpose.
2. **Creative Commons Attribution (CC BY)**—This means anyone can use the work in question for any purpose—even for commercial projects—as long as they credit the original creator and provide a link to the original.
3. **Creative Commons Attribution-ShareAlike (CC BY-SA)**—Like the CC BY license, this license means anyone can use the media in question for any purpose—even commercially—as long as they credit the original creator,

provide a link to the original, and release their work under the CC BY-SA license, too.

Wikimedia Commons, like Wikipedia itself, takes copyright seriously, so only upload images that either you created or you can prove were released under a compatible license. Be warned: most images you find on the internet were not released under this sort of license (simply because an image is online does not mean it is free to use). And although the Army of the Potomac is unlikely to kick down your door and arrest you if you upload a copyrighted image to Wikimedia Commons, this sort of behavior could earn you a stern talking-to from an admin; if you continue this sort of behavior, you might even be banned from editing.

For those new to Wikimedia Commons, the upload process is as follows:

1. Locate the image that you want to upload. Save it to your computer, making note of who made it, where you got it, and what its license is.
2. Go to **Wikimedia Commons** (https://commons.wikimedia.org/wiki/Main_Page) and log in using your Wikipedia username and password.
3. On the far left-hand side of the main screen, choose the option that says **Upload file**.
4. This will take you to the **Upload Wizard** page. From here, click **Select media files to share**. Select the image from your computer and click **Open**.
5. The **Upload** process will begin immediately. Once the image has successfully been uploaded to the server, click **Continue**.
6. Now you will be taken to the **Release rights** tab. Here, you will need to explain where the image came from:
    a. If you created it, select **This file is my own work**.
        i. You will then be asked to digitally certify that you are releasing the work through a Creative Commons license. Click **Next**.
    b. If you found it elsewhere, select **This file is not my own work**.
        i. You will need to specify the image's **Source** and its **Author**.
        ii. You will then be asked to specify under what license the image has been released. When you are finished, click **Next**.
7. This will take you to the **Describe** tab. Specify the image's source (where you found it, such as a URL), the author(s) of the image, and its license.
8. Next, you will need to provide the image with a **Title**, a **Caption** (a short, one-line summary of the image), and a **Description** (a more detailed explanation of what the image depicts).[17] Then, specify the **Date** that work was created or published.
9. You can also add a **Category**, if you know one off the top of your head. (For instance, if I were uploading an image of the Lawrence, Kansas, public library, I could type "Public libraries in Kansas" in the Category box.) This step, however, is optional.

10. Once all the fields have been filled out, click **Publish files**.
11. This will take you to the **Add data** tab, which allows you to tag items in your upload. This step is also optional.
12. Next, click **Publish data for all files.** This will take you to the **Use** tab.
13. To add the image to an article on Wikipedia, follow the steps outlined on pages 61–62. When prompted to search for an image, type in the exact name or title of the file you just uploaded.

If the upload process seems too daunting, you can also visit Wikipedia:Files for upload on Wikipedia. On this page, users can request image uploads from more seasoned editors. Not every request will be filled, but it never hurts to ask.

Table 5.4. Suggestions for Further Reading

"Designing a Media Contribution Assignment." Wiki Education, accessed July 27, 2021. https://dashboard.wikiedu.org/training/instructors/illustration-assignment.
"How to Upload Images to Wikimedia Commons." Wikimedia Guide, March 2019. https://upload.wikimedia.org/wikipedia/commons/0/0d/How_to_Upload_Images_ to_Wikimedia_Commons.pdf.
Ross, Sage. *Illustrating Wikipedia: A Guide to Contributing Content to Wikimedia Commons.* San Francisco: Wikimedia Foundation, 2013. http://education.wikimedia .org/illustrating.

ACCESSIBILITY CONSIDERATIONS

A topic often neglected when discussing ways to improve Wikipedia is accessibility. This term refers to the way individuals can "[make a] website, with all of its data and functions, available for anyone, no matter how they have to use [the] website, or what difficulties they might have."[18] Many erroneously assume that because Wikipedia is mostly text, it is already accessible. The truth, however, is that many of the site's articles have accessibility problems that need to be fixed.

One of the more persistent issues is the use of low-contrast colors in tables and templates; this is especially an issue when colored text is set against a colored background. Sometimes, the contrast between colored text and background (such as lime green [hex code #32CD32] text over a bright yellow [#FFFF00] background) is so low that almost all users, regardless of visual acuity, have trouble understanding what is going on. Other schemes (such as red [#FFFF00] text over a green [#32CD32] background) might appear readable to most users but are nevertheless difficult to read for those who are colorblind. To ensure that the site is visually accessible to the widest possible audience, Wikipedia requires that all color schemes have a contrast ratio of at least 4.5:1

(in other words, one color must be 4.5 times brighter than the other); if a higher ratio between the two colors can be achieved, all the better. To measure the contrast ratio between two colors, an editor can use the WebAIM's "Contrast Checker." This tool allows an editor to enter the hex codes for two different colors; the tool will then display the contrast ratio between the two colors, indicating whether the ratio is above 4.5:1.[19]

Another accessibility issue has to do with Wikipedia's images. For most readers, an image in an article can nicely supplement its content. But for those who are visually impaired or use text-to-speech programs to access articles, images alone are an inappropriate means to convey information. To fix this issue, editors can add alternative text (often called "alt-text") to images. In simple terms, "alt-text" can be understood as a detailed description of an image, which can be detected and read aloud by text-to-speech programs. This offers people the ability to perceive in their mind an image that they might not be able to literally visualize.[20] To add alt-text to an image using the Visual Editor, the steps are as follows:

1. Click on the **Edit** button, either at the top of the Wikipedia page, or at the start of the section in which the image is located.
2. Click on the image in question; this will cause an **Image** pop-up box to appear.
3. From this box, click the **Edit** button.
4. In the **Alternative text** slot, provide a brief description of the image.
5. When you have added the necessary alt-text, click on **Apply changes** option.

If you are using the plain text editor, the steps will be slightly different:

1. Click on the **Edit source** button, either at the top of the Wikipedia page, or at the start of the section in which the image is located.
2. Navigate to the image in the source code. It might, for instance, look like this:

   ```
   [[File:ThisIsASample.jpg|thumb|350px|Here is a sam-
   ple image]]
   ```

3. Place your cursor at the end of the image description, but before the closing brackets. Then, type a vertical bar (|) followed by `alt=` and a detailed alt-text description of the image. It should look something like this:

   ```
   [[File:ThisIsASample.jpg|thumb|350px|Here is a sam-
   ple image|alt=This is an example of alt text]]
   ```

4. When finished, click **Publish changes**.

Once the article is updated, text-to-speech programs will be able to read the alt-text description, providing context for those who need it.

If you are interested in accessibility concerns, you might consider joining the "Accessibility" WikiProject (located at Wikipedia:WikiProject Accessibility). This group will not only introduce you to like-minded editors, but also lead you to accessibility-focused resources that can be used when you edit.

Table 5.5. Suggestions for Further Reading

Cunningham, Katie. *Accessibility Handbook: Making 508 Websites for Everyone.* Sebastopol, CA: O'Reilly, 2012.

"Wikipedia:Accessibility dos and don'ts." Wikipedia, accessed July 27, 2021. https://en.wikipedia.org/w/index.php?title=Wikipedia:Accessibility_dos_and_don%27ts&oldid=995313349.

"Wikipedia:Manual of Style/Accessibility." Wikipedia, accessed July 27, 2021. https://en.wikipedia.org/w/index.php?title=Wikipedia:Manual_of_Style/Accessibility&oldid=1032725833.

HOSTING EDIT-A-THONS

After you have gained experience working with Wikipedia, a more advanced way to help improve the site is by hosting an "edit-a-thon." These are events in which groups of people meet and edit Wikipedia together in person. Edit-a-thons are useful because they leverage concentrated attention and the power of many to improve the site's coverage of specific topics. What follows is a step-by-step guide to hosting an edit-a-thon, replete with "best practices" to ensure that your event is successful.

Step 1: Set a Goal and Theme for the Event—Many edit-a-thon veterans have stressed the importance of establishing a goal for your event.[21] Ask yourself: What exactly is it that you hope to accomplish with the edit-a-thon? Do you want participants to focus largely on copyediting, or will they be creating articles from scratch? Do you hope to make a certain number of edits as a group? Do you hope to expand a certain number of articles? Establishing explicit goals such as these can be especially useful when working with newcomers, as many might not know what is expected of them.[22]

Closely related to an event's goal is the event's theme. To determine your theme, think about what area of Wikipedia you hope to improve. Of course, nothing is wrong with a group of editors meeting to edit widely disparate articles that interest them. However, this sort of ad hoc approach often fails to make systemic changes, as editors are scattered and not working together as a unit. A clear theme also makes it easier to attract participants—especially those with a very specific knowledge base. In the past, prominent edit-a-thons have been themed around improving Wikipedia's coverage of LGBTQ+ topics, notable women, climate change science, medicine, and non-Western cultures, to name just a few.

Step 2: Determine Event Logistics—One logistical hurdle you are likely to face is the issue of space: Where will the edit-a-thon be hosted?[23] To answer this question, first determine how many people you think will attend your event. If you expect only a handful of participants, it is wise to choose a space that would allow for a more intimate experience, such as a coffee shop. But if you think several dozen people might show up, consider a larger space that can comfortably accommodate a crowd. You will also need to ensure that your location has adequate internet access, and it is recommended that you choose a location that has public computer stations, so that those who do not own computers can still participate. Given that most have large meeting rooms, free Wi-Fi, and public computer access, libraries are excellent places to host edit-a-thons. Libraries are also a smart choice because they house books and other reference materials that editors can use to improve Wikipedia. Other spaces conducive to edit-a-thons include museums, art galleries, and college facilities.

Another hurdle that edit-a-thon organizers face is the problem of account registering. Although anyone is free to create a Wikipedia account, only six accounts can be created a day per IP address. This means that if fifty editor-hopefuls come to your edit-a-thon and need to create accounts, forty-four will be left out in the cold. The easiest solution to prevent a problem such as this is to organize your event through Wikimedia's "Programs & Events Dashboard," which allows you to create new accounts without limit (a step-by-step guide to creating an edit-a-thon using this tool can be found at meta:Programs & Events Dashboard/Using the Dashboard).

Another option is to request that all edit-a-thon participants create an account prior to the event; this ensures that on the day of the edit-a-thon, all editor accounts are set up and ready to go. (Of note, participants who hope to create new articles need to have had their account for at least four days and have made at least ten edits—which is another reason to encourage partici-pants to create an account prior to the event.)[24] Having said all this, remember, a registered account is not required to edit Wikipedia; if fifty editor-hopefuls show up and do not have accounts, they can always edit the site anonymously (although their privileges will be limited).

If, in the course of organizing an edit-a-thon, you find yourself in need of capital to reserve a location space, rent tech equipment, or even secure short-term babysitting services, Wikimedia offers a "Rapid Fund" program,[25] which grants funding between $500 and $2,000 for "short-term, low-cost projects by individuals, groups, or organizations contributing to Wikimedia projects."[26] Note that grant requests go through an application process, and those who seek funding need to have an established history of contributing to Wikipedia.

Step 3: Advertise the Event—Solid turnout is key to a successful edit-a-thon. For best results, the organizer of an edit-a-thon is encouraged to embrace a three-pronged advertising approach: first, contact people in your immediate community; then reach out to people on Wikipedia; and finally, drum up interest by sending a message through all other digital avenues.

The first group of people you should reach out to are those from your local community who you think might be an asset to the event. If you are hosting your edit-a-thon at a research library or a university, send a message to faculty or staff members who might be able to lend you a hand vis-à-vis their expertise; after all, a distinguished professor of history is a great resource if you are hosting a history-focused edit-a-thon. Sometimes professors and other instructors will even advertise edit-a-thons in their classes, encouraging students to drop by (sometimes promising extra credit to those who turn out).

Second, advertise your event on Wikipedia by reaching out to editors whose editing history aligns with the theme of your event; for instance, if you hope to improve coverage about the indigenous peoples of Central America, think about connecting with the editors who are active in the "Mesoamerica"[27] or "Indigenous peoples of the Americas"[28] WikiProjects. You could also message the *Signpost*, Wikipedia's digital newsletter, about your upcoming event.[29] Given sufficient notice, the *Signpost* might be able to feature your event and boost digital attendance.

Finally, it would behoove you to use the vast, digital world to your advantage. Post about your event on social media platforms such as Facebook, Twitter, or Instagram. If you have a blog, publish a post or two. E-mail friends and colleagues from other institutions, or send a message to relevant mailing lists. In these messages, it is important to include detailed information about the "when," "where," and "why" of the event. Also include contact information so that people can reach out if they have questions.

Step 4: Teach Participants How to Edit—Although some people who come to an edit-a-thon might already have experience working with Wikipedia, it is likely that for many, this will be their first time in the editor role. It is thus prudent, if not essential, to hold a workshop during the edit-a-thon that covers Wikipedia's policies as well as the basics of editing. The exact specifics of this workshop are ultimately up to the event organizer. For instance, in edit-a-thons that I have organized, I like to host an introductory "how to" workshop at the start of the event so that from the beginning everyone is on the same page. Other organizers prefer to hold mini-workshops over the course of their edit-a-thons, with each workshop dedicated to a specific topic (e.g., how to add a picture to an article, how to insert citations).[30] Regardless of the specifics, the emphasis of these workshops should always be on educating users, new and old alike, by providing them with the necessary tools needed to make Wikipedia better.

Demonstrating the capabilities of Wikipedia by means of the user sandbox feature is an excellent way to get newer editors up to speed; because an editor's sandbox is ultimately controlled by the editor in question, it functions as a "home base" where they can play around with Wikipedia's many editing tools. This allows editors to get a feel for the site without fearing that their work will be erased or interfered with by more seasoned editors. Many organizers also find it useful to provide participants with a "cheat sheet"[31] that covers Wikipedia's policies or the way its markup language works (such as the one featured in chapter 4); this enables new editors to better help themselves in times of confusion, thereby boosting their self-esteem and encouraging them to continue editing on their own.

Step 5: Oversee Editing—The final aspect of the edit-a-thon is the actual process of editing Wikipedia. If you are leading an edit-a-thon, it is generally recommended that you oversee the other participants, ensuring that any questions they raise are answered in a timely manner. If participants are unsure as to what they ought to be editing, you can always serve as a wiki-adviser by suggesting articles that you know need to be expanded or cleaned up. And of course, you are encouraged to edit alongside everyone else.

If you hope to jot down statistics about the event, you can do it in a variety of ways. Perhaps the simplest method is to use a sign-in sheet, on which participants can jot down basic information: name, Wikipedia username, and any articles that they modified. The problem with this method, however, is that it relies on self-reporting and can thus be a bit inaccurate. More complex options include the Event Metrics dashboard[32] or Wiki Education's Programs and Events Dashboard[33]—both of which are Web resources that can be accessed with a Wikipedia username and password. These sites allow you to set up a page for your specific event, keep track of all the Wikipedia users who are involved, and then analyze the edits made by the edit-a-thon's participants. Remember, if you plan to collect and analyze this sort of data, you will need the participants' consent first.

Table 5.6. Suggestions for Further Reading

Mabey, Jacqueline. *Art+Feminism: Quick Guide for Organizers*. San Francisco: Wikimedia Foundation, 2020.

Triumph, Therese, F., and Kimberley M. Henze. "Women and Wikipedia: Diversifying Editors and Enhancing Content through Library Edit-a-Thons." In *Gender Issues and the Library: Case Studies of Innovative Programs and Resources*, edited by Carol Smallwood and Lura Sanborn, 155–62. Jefferson, NC: McFarland, 2017.

Wiki Education. "Running Editathons and Other Editing Events." Wiki Education, accessed October 19, 2021. https://outreachdashboard.wmflabs.org/training/editathons.

"Wikipedia:How to run an edit-a-thon." Wikipedia, accessed July 27, 2021. https://en.wikipedia.org/w/index.php?title=Wikipedia:How_to_run_an_edit-a-thon&oldid=1035490044.

GLAMORIZING WIKIPEDIA: WORKING WITH GALLERIES, LIBRARIES, ARCHIVES, AND MUSEUMS

So far, the methods discussed in this chapter have been aimed at the average editor. In this section, however, I want to turn my attention specifically to individuals who work in cultural institutions such as galleries, libraries, archives, or museums (GLAMs). Such professionals are a boon to Wikipedia because the institutions with which they are affiliated usually house valuable resources—rare books, manuscripts, paintings, and photographs—that can be digitized and used to improve the site. This is a win-win situation, for it not only makes Wikipedia more comprehensive, but also boosts a cultural institution's digital presence.

On Wikipedia, the main group spearheading collaboration between Wikipedia and cultural institutions is the aptly named GLAM-Wiki initiative. This project began in 2008 when Liam Wyatt, an Australian editor, suggested that Wikipedia reach out and work with cultural institutions such as libraries and museums. After Wyatt organized a conference based on this idea, titled "Galleries, Libraries, Archives, Museums & Wikimedia: Finding the Common Ground," the fledgling GLAM-Wiki project began to coalesce into something more "official."[34]

In time, members of the GLAM-Wiki began reaching out to cultural institutions across the globe, inquiring if they were interested in working with Wikipedia to openly share their special collections online. Some institutions were understandably reluctant to collaborate with pseudonymous editors, but others—such as the British Museum and the U.S. National Archives and Records Administration[35]—enthusiastically agreed.[36] This project has continued to grow, and as of 2021, GLAM-Wiki has worked with hundreds of institutions to expand more than 2,000 articles and upload more than 194,000 images.[37] And of GLAM-Wiki's many initiatives, one of the more unique projects is the "Wikipedian in Residence" arrangement, which pairs a Wikipedia editor with an established GLAM institution. The editor then works closely with that institution to create articles "related to that institution's mission, encourage and assist it to release material under open [licenses], and to develop the relationship between the host institution and the Wikimedia community."[38]

GLAM-Wiki has done great things, but one way in which the initiative could grow is by increasing its efforts to work with small or rural cultural institutions such as county museums or libraries, or volunteer-run historical societies. On their own, these organizations might not be as culturally impactful as something like the Library of Congress, but they nevertheless account for a sizable portion of the world's cultural institutions. (The United States alone, for instance, has more than 35,144 museums, of which 43 percent are in small or rural communities.[39] Likewise, a report by the Institute of Museum and Library Services reveals that the United States has 9,057 public libraries, of which

4,002 are classified as rural libraries.)[40] Many of these institutions house the cultural memory of small, often overlooked communities, whose histories are largely unknown to outsiders. Unfortunately, Wiki-GLAM has not focused near as much energy on these collections, and because of this neglect, a real possibility is that the unique resources of these minor institutions—for example, church records, old newspapers, community histories, yearbooks, photographs, microfiche—may one day be lost to the sands of time.

It is important to stress that this neglect is not due to a problem with GLAM-Wiki's guiding ethos. Instead, it is simply an unfortunate result of the volunteer-based system upon which the entire Wikipedia project is run. Because GLAM-Wiki cannot possibly work with all cultural institutions, its members tend to prioritize collaborations with larger organizations, whose holdings are often vast and notable, making it worth the time and effort it takes to secure them. The same cannot always be said about many minor museums and libraries, whose resources, although undoubtedly important, are usually small and not the most in demand. Another issue is that minor institutions often do not have the resources or the technical know-how to host large-scale digitization projects, edit-a-thons, residency programs, and so forth. If you are a Wikipedia editor interested in preserving cultural memory, think about the minor GLAM institutions in your area. Consider reaching out to see if they would be interested in uploading some of their holdings to Wikimedia Commons, or using their historical documents to better reference Wikipedia articles.

#1LIB1REF

Another way GLAM institutions can help make Wikipedia better is by participating in the #1lib1ref campaign. Deriving its name from the phrase "one librarian, one reference," this event—held twice a year, from January 15 to February 5 and from May 15 to June 5—encourages librarians and other information professionals to add a reference to Wikipedia, providing much-needed sourcing. Similar in many ways to an edit-a-thon, the #1lib1ref project was based on the idea that "many hands make light work." It was developed by Alex Stinson, project manager of the Wikipedia Library, specifically to "[increase] literacy and understanding among librarians about how Wikipedia's content is created and improved through verifiability."[41]

Participating in the #1lib1ref campaign is rather simple, with the campaign's official Wikimedia page breaking it all down into five steps:

1. First, a librarian is to find an article that needs a citation. To make this task easier, the organizers of #1lib1ref suggest that participants use Citation Hunt,[42] a Web-based tool that scans Wikipedia at random and finds an article with the infamous [citation needed] tag, indicating that a statement is in need of a source.[43] (For those new to Wikipedia who do not want to be

thrown into the metaphorical deep end just yet, Citation Hunt also allows editors to key in a specific topic, allowing them to stick to articles about which they might be more familiar.)

2. The librarian then must verify that the statement is true and find a reliable source to add to the article. (If the unsourced statement is *not* true or appears to be original research, it should be culled immediately.) This step is perhaps the trickiest because it requires participants to verify information and track down sourcing. Thankfully, this is a task at which librarians and other information professionals often excel. In their quest to verify and cite, many participants pore over reference materials from their own institutions, whereas others turn to online databases such as JSTOR or PubMed. And still others might scour book archives such as Google Books or Archive.org.[44] Whatever method works best for you, it is important that you use reputable, scholarly, and rigorous resources.

3. The librarian is then to edit the page, remove the [citation needed] tag, and replace it with a Wikipedia-formatted citation (for a refresher on this process, see chapters 3 and 4).

4. When saving the page, the librarian should add `#1lib1ref` in the **Edit summary** box. This will allow the 1lib1ref number-crunchers to include your edit when they tabulate the campaign's outcomes. (Try your hardest to remember this step, but do not fret if you forget. Remember: hashtag or not, participation is what really matters.)

5. Finally, the librarian is encouraged to share their contribution via social media along with the hashtag "#1lib1ref." This helps to spread the word and encourages other librarians and information professionals to take part, too.

Although the #1lib1ref campaign might be relatively new in the grand scheme of Wikipedia's history, its results speak for themselves: in its inaugural year, the campaign saw 228 editors on the English Wikipedia make at least 907 edits on 671 pages.[45] In comparison, the 2021 campaign saw 386 users make 10,416 edits to 4,155 pages on the English Wikipedia.[46] If librarians can keep up this good work and spread the word, the #1lib1ref campaign will likely continue to make a difference.

BRINGING WIKIPEDIA INTO THE CLASSROOM

Despite the common assumption that Wikipedia is the bane of every teacher, it is becoming more common to hear of instructors who bring Wikipedia into their classroom. This can be done in many ways—for instance, some instructors have students copyedit pages, translate articles, or upload images[47]—but arguably the most popular method is to have students write original articles for inclusion on the site. This might sound easy enough, but for students who have had little to no training on how Wikipedia works, assigning such a project can be a logistical nightmare that results only in frustration.

To head off problems like this, it is recommended that instructors interested in bringing Wikipedia into their classroom work closely with Wiki Education (a nonprofit organization focused on constructively bringing Wikipedia into the higher education classroom in the United States and Canada)[48] to develop suitable assignments for their classes. One of the many projects that Wiki Education runs is the Wikipedia Student Program, which facilitates the article-creation process by providing resources and training to ensure that all participants understand the project. The Wikipedia Student Program also makes an instructor's life easier by providing a digital "Dashboard" to keep track of all the articles that their students are creating. (The Wikipedia Student Program also requires instructors to take part in an online Wikipedia orientation module before their classroom project begins, ensuring that faculty who are interested in Wikipedia but not familiar with the inner workings of the site can be brought up to speed quickly.)[49]

If you are interested in having Wiki Education help you design a project, you can submit an application at https://teach.wikiedu.org/. (Wiki Education's willingness to work with classes and help guide content creation has produced some remarkable content. According to LiAnna Davis, Wiki Education's chief programs officer, "Since 2010, Wiki Education has supported more than 4,800 classes who have incorporated editing assignments. More than 97,000 students have edited through our program, adding more than 80 million words to 109,000 Wikipedia articles. [In this way] we also bring 19% of all the new active editors to English Wikipedia."[50] Those are quite the numbers.)

Students can create articles in a variety of ways, but my experience in the classroom leads me to believe that these kinds of projects are most successful when they follow a clearly structured plan of action, such as the one that follows:

Step 1: Acclimating Students to Wikipedia—Because many students are not aware of how Wikipedia content is edited, an instructor should first introduce students to the basics of editing. First, show students how an ideal Wikipedia article is arranged. Explain that the lead section of an article functions as a summary of the article's body, and that the body itself is often divided into distinct sections. Point out the way Wikipedia uses footnotes to cite facts, and use this as an opportunity to emphasize that every assertion on the site needs to be backed up by a reliable source. At this point, I find it helpful also to explain the nature of encyclopedic writing. (Thanks to years of traditional education, most students have come to believe that anything they write needs to be catchy and persuasive, but this kind of writing is not appropriate for Wikipedia.) Discuss how Wikipedia differs from a traditional essay, stressing that Wikipedia articles should strive for neutrality by always referring back to what has been said in published sources.

Next, have students create their own accounts. (If you are helming this project by yourself, remember that only six accounts can be created per IP address per day, meaning that it might be best to stagger the creation of accounts or assign the task as homework.)[51] If you are working with Wiki Education, your students will then have to take a few training modules that introduce them to the basics of Wikipedia editing. It can also be helpful to discuss in person the way editing works. You do not want to confuse students, so it is best to start with the basics of the Visual Editor (e.g., What button do you click to edit an article? How do you make text bold/italicized?). When your class is comfortable with the Visual Editor interface, introduce them to the plain text editor and the specifics of wikitext.

Step 2: Assigning Articles—The next step is to match a student with a topic for a prospective article. One way to do this is to have the students themselves identify a topic of interest that they could flesh out into a new article. This provides the students with flexibility and freedom to write about what interests them. Unfortunately, students often struggle when told to find articles that *don't* exist, and for this reason, it might be best if you curate a list of potential topics that students can work on; this narrows the scope of the assignment and reduces student anxiety about choosing the "right" topic.[52] Some instructors choose to simplify this project even further by asking students to improve underdeveloped articles, rather than create new ones. Wikipedia, after all, is littered with myriad "stub" and "start" articles just begging for improvement. Having students expand articles is an especially good option for a class on a short timetable.[53] For a list of articles in need of expansion, see Category: Articles to be expanded or Wikipedia:Maintenance#Article_expansion.

Step 3: Drafting Articles—With accounts created and articles assigned, it is time for students to begin researching and writing their articles. Until an article is ready to be published in the mainspace of Wikipedia, it is best to confine article writing to a user's sandbox. (Keeping the article in a sandbox for a time ensures that other editors will see it as a draft, meaning they are less likely to interfere with the student's effort. This seclusion often makes students feel more at ease and willing to experiment with writing and formatting.) Show students where they can find their sandbox feature and explain its functionality. Let the students know that the first few passes of their article can be a bit messy, as they are drafts, but stress that under no circumstance should students simply copy and paste content from one site into their sandbox with no attribution (as such an act could constitute plagiarism as well as copyright infringement).

Step 4: Submitting Articles for Review—Once a student has finished an article, they will notify their instructor. The instructor will then read the article draft, making minor edits where necessary and documenting more glaring issues that the student will be expected to fix—a process that is, in many ways, analogous to scholarly peer review. When the review is complete, the student will receive the instructor's comments. If the article is of quality, it will be published, but if it has issues that need to be fixed, the student will be asked to revise and resubmit their work.

Step 5: Publishing Articles: Once the instructor has approved a student's article, the final step is for the student to publish the article to the Wikipedia mainspace. To do this, a student will need to:

1. Go to their **sandbox**, and from the upper right-hand corner of the screen, select the option that says **More**.
2. From this drop-down menu, select **Move**.
3. This will take the student to the **Move page form**:
   a. From the drop-down menu under **New title**, change **User** to **(Article)**
   b. In the box next to the drop-down menu, type in the final name of the article. Remember to use sentence case.
   c. In the **Reason** box, type a variation of "Creating new article."
   d. Click **Move page**. This will move the student's completed article from their sandbox onto the mainspace of Wikipedia.

Now, anyone with access to the site can find the student's newly created article by simply typing its title in the search bar.

Step 6: Seeking Post-Publication Review—After the articles go live, it can be a good idea to have students reach out to other Wikipedia editors and see if they have any thoughts about the new articles. (Some editors might even be willing to provide an additional round of constructive criticism.) Having students seek out post-publication review not only ensures that their articles will undergo additional scrutiny, but also encourages students to remain active on Wikipedia after their assignment is, for all intents and purposes, finished.

If you are interested in a more detail-oriented outline for a project like the one just discussed, Wiki Education has created a useful syllabus for a twelve-week Wikipedia unit, which has been included in the "Suggestions for Further Research" box below. This syllabus expands on many of the steps discussed in this section, suggesting additional readings, an ideal time line, and a grading structure. Wiki Education has also created a variety of tutorials for both students and educators that detail Wikipedia's many intricacies; these modules can be accessed on the organization's "Training Libraries" webpage (https://dashboard.wikiedu.org/training).

Table 5.7. Suggestions for Further Reading

Davis, LiAnna. *Case Studies: How Professors Are Teaching with Wikipedia*. San Francisco: Wikimedia Foundation, 2012. http://education.wikimedia.org/casestudies.

———. *Instructor Basics: How to Use Wikipedia as a Teaching Tool*. San Francisco: Wikimedia Foundation, 2012. http://education.wikimedia.org/instructorbasics.

Fenoll, Carme, John Cummings, Jesús Tramullas, and Àlex Hinojo. *Opportunities for Public Libraries and Wikipedia*. International Federation of Library Associations and Institutions and The Wikipedia Library, 2016. http://eprints.rclis.org/39905/1/iflawikipediaandpubliclibraries.pdf.

Wiki Education. "Designing a Wikipedia Writing and Research Assignment." Wiki Education, accessed October 19, 2021. https://dashboard.wikiedu.org/training/instructors/designing-a-writing-assignment.

Wikipedia:GLAM/Bookshelf." Wikipedia, accessed July 27, 2021. https://en.wikipedia.org/w/index.php?title=Wikipedia:GLAM/Bookshelf&oldid=1029801910.

"The Wikipedia Library/1Lib1Ref." Wikimedia, accessed July 27, 2021. https://meta.wikimedia.org/w/index.php?title=The_Wikipedia_Library/1Lib1Ref&oldid=21381500.

6

Becoming a Critical Editor

Countering Bias

As I have touched on a few times already in this book, one of Wikipedia's strongest assets is its size and scope: the English site by itself comprises well more than six million articles, and when all language variants are counted, that number swells to a staggering fifty-seven million articles. The entire project is easily one of the largest collections of information ever assembled. But shockingly, despite its massive size, the site still has glaring omissions, which often align with the systemic inequalities of our world; articles about marginalized peoples and cultures, for instance, are less common than articles about systemically privileged peoples and cultures. And even when articles about marginalized topics do exist, they tend to be more rudimentarily developed when compared to articles that cover similar, albeit "popular" topics. To put it simply, Wikipedia's coverage of knowledge is structurally biased.

The claim that Wikipedia is prejudiced is not a new one—*The Guardian* ran a piece about Wikipedia's skewed coverage of geographic topics back in 2009,[1] and a year later, a prominent Wikipedia survey prompted increasing discussions about gender disparity on the site.[2] But it is one that still demands our attention. Unfortunately, many overviews of the site either downplay the problem of bias, cover it up with overly utopic language about the site's wonders, or ignore it completely. Given that Wikipedia's skewed coverage can very literally impact how people understand the world, sidestepping or ignoring its bias is unacceptable.

For this reason, I have chosen to focus the final chapter in this book on the problem of bias. I will list and discuss the ways these problems have emerged and how they skew article coverage. I will then introduce a new way of looking at Wikipedia, which I call "critical editing." Using the critical editing framework, I will explicate ways that users can read and contribute to articles in a critical way that (ideally) cuts down on the site's biases.

GENDER BIAS

Of the many biases that plague Wikipedia, perhaps the most infamous is the "gender gap." Many studies suggest that far more men edit the site than women, and articles about women tend to be shorter than those about men. Regarding the former problem, a 2011 survey of Wikipedia conducted by the Wikimedia Foundation reported that 91 percent of those who contributed to the site identified as male, compared to the 8.5 percent who identified as female.[3] A Wikimedia report issued in 2018 showed that effectively no progress had been made to close this gap, with 90 percent of editors identifying as male and 8.8 percent identifying as female.[4] On top of these already troubling statistics, evidence shows that, when compared to their male counterparts, female editors are more likely to stop contributing to the site prematurely.[5]

Why are there fewer women editors? It is a good question, one that has puzzled scholars for some time now. One possible answer is that many of Wikipedia's more dedicated editors have a background in programming and computer science. Because men are already overrepresented in these fields, it is reasonable to assume that men would be overrepresented among Wikipedia editors, too. Another hypothesis has to do with gender roles and expectations about what men and women should and should not do. In many cultures (especially Western ones) women have, by and large, been socialized to avoid conflict. Unfortunately—as anyone who has gotten into an edit war or a talk page debate can tell you—much of Wikipedia's culture revolves around spirited and sometimes heated debate between editors. Thanks to this "climate of conflict," women may be less inclined to take part in a project, given that it is at least in part predicated on behavior that they have been enculturated to avoid.

But Wikipedia's gender bias runs deeper than just lopsided editor demographics. This is readily apparent when you consider the site's coverage—or lack thereof—of gendered content. According to a 2011 study by Joseph Reagle and Lauren Rhue, for instance, "Wikipedia articles on women are more likely to be missing than are articles on men relative to *Britannica*."[6] (Less than 20 percent of biographies on the site are about women, for instance.) And of those articles that do focus or discuss women, many are much shorter than comparable articles about men.[7] In 2013, Tom Simonite made a similar point when he demonstrated that "articles worked on mostly by female editors—which presumably were more likely to be of interest to women—were significantly shorter than those worked on mostly by male editors or by men and women equally";[8] later that same year, Simonite's points were echoed by a study released by Shyong K. Lam, Anuradha Uduwage, Zhenhua, et al., who used statistical analyses to show that "articles about 'female' movies are shorter than ones about 'male' movies."[9]

But to my mind, the most alarming evidence of gender bias in Wikipedia's content can be found in a 2016 paper by Claudia Wagner, Eduardo

Graells-Garrido, David Garcia, and Filippo Menczer, in which the authors demonstrated that, on average, "women in Wikipedia are 13% more notable[10] than their male counterparts."[11] Although this might sound like a good thing at first, it means that editors are more likely to reject a biographical article as "non-notable" if it is about a woman. In other words, women are—often unconsciously—held to a higher standard than men when it comes to the metrics for inclusion. Unfortunately, little has changed in this regard, and a 2021 study by Francesca Tripodi argued that "women's biographies are [still] more frequently miscategorized as non-notable than men's."[12]

Thankfully, several projects are pushing back against this gender bias, of which the most successful is arguably the "Women in Red" WikiProject. The purpose of this project is to counter the "systemic bias [against] women's biographies . . . and their works—broadly construed" by encouraging the targeted editing of articles about women.[13] The project was formed in 2015 under the name "WikiProject XX" (a play on the now-defunct "WikiProject X" that alludes to the two X chromosomes belonging to the homogametic sex), although its name was soon changed to "Women in Red" to avoid accusations of gender essentialism.[14]

The name "Women in Red" itself was popularized by User:T. Anthony, who kept a running list on his user page of notable women that otherwise lacked Wikipedia articles; because these biographical articles did not exist, links to them would appear as red links, hence the project's eventual name.[15] By adopting T. Anthony's turn of phrase as its name, the Women in Red WikiProject made it clear that their mission was to "turn women blue"—that is, create pages for notable women so that links to those articles would appear as valid wikilinks. Since 2015, the Women in Red WikiProject has facilitated the creation of 167,423 biographical articles about women, helping to raise the percentage of articles about women from 15.5 percent in 2015 to a little more than 19 percent as of August 2021.[16]

Another group helping to bridge the gender gap is the Art+Feminism initiative, which aims to improve Wikipedia's coverage of female artists via targeted edit-a-thons. Art+Feminism can trace its roots back to 2013, when a group of academics, artists, and curators that included Siân Evans, Jacqueline Mabey, Michael Mandiberg, and Laurel Ptak came together to improve Wikipedia's coverage of female artists and creative feminist expression.[17] Only about one hundred people took part in the group's 2014 edit-a-thon, but the following year, that number ballooned to thirteen hundred. Since then, Art+Feminism has made a noticeable impact on the site, having helped eighteen thousand editors create or improve well over eighty-four thousand articles about female artists.[18]

Despite all the great work done by projects such as Women in Red or Art+Feminism, many areas still need improvement. The number of male editors, after all, still drastically outweighs the number of non-male editors, and the site is still overflowing with articles about men. Lesser-discussed but equally important issues include the dearth of articles comprehensively discussing trans, nonbinary, genderfluid, and intersex individuals, as well as the use in articles of gendered terms that assume maleness is the "default" mode of existence.

"GLOBAL NORTH" BIAS

Another bias impacting Wikipedia is the disproportionate focus on what many call the "Global North," defined here as those "countries found mainly, but not exclusively, in the northern hemisphere, characterized by high levels of economic development."[19] Comprising the United States, Canada, Europe, Oceania, and Japan, this bloc of countries stands in contrast to (and often overshadows) the "Global South," or "the countries of Africa, Central and Latin America, and most of Asia [which largely] have emerging economies."[20] One way to see this Global North bias is by looking at the popularity of Wikipedia's myriad language editions. Of the hundreds that exist, the ten largest (in terms of human-created articles)[21] at the start of 2019 were as follows:

Table 6.1. Ten Largest Wikipedias (2019)

Rank	Language	Articles (of 33.1 million)	Percentage of All Wikipedia Articles	Percentage of World Speaks That Language
1	English	5.6 million	16.92%	14.73%
2	German	2.3 million	6.95%	1.72%
3	French	2 million	6.04%	3.63%
4	Spanish	1.5 million	4.53%	6.95%
5	Russian	1.4 million	4.23%	3.35%
6	Italian	1.4 million	4.23%	0.89%
7	Polish	1.2 million	3.63%	0.52%
8	Japanese	1.1 million	3.32%	1.67%
9	Dutch	0.91 million	2.74%	0.30%
10	Mandarin	0.88 million	2.65%	14.51%

Sources: Wikimedia Foundation, "Wikipedia Statistics"; *Ethnologue*, "What Are the Top 200 Most Spoken Languages?" 2019, archived at https://w.wiki.5Bh3; and World Bank, "Population, Total" [2019], https://data.worldbank.org/indicator/SP.POP.TOTL.

Now compare these numbers to the ten most widely spoken languages (taking into account both first- and second-language speakers) at the start of 2019:

Table 6.2. Most Widely Spoken Languages (2019)

Rank	Language	Speakers (of 7.683 billion)	Percentage of World Speaks That Language
1	English	1.132 billion	14.73%
2	Mandarin	1.115 billion	14.51%
3	Hindi	615 million	8.00%
4	Spanish	534 million	6.95%
5	French	279 million	3.63%
6	Standard Arabic	273 million	3.55%
7	Bengali	265 million	3.45%
8	Russian	258 million	3.36%
9	Portuguese	234 million	3.05%
10	Indonesian	199 million	2.59%

Sources: *Ethnologue*, "What Are the Top 200 Most Spoken Languages?" 2019, archived at https://w.wiki/5Bh3; and World Bank, "Population, Total" [2019], https://data.worldbank.org/indicator/SP.POP.TOTL.

One would expect that the more widely spoken a language, the bigger its edition of Wikipedia would be, but this is not what we see. Instead, many of the biggest Wikipedia editions in 2019 were written in languages common to or spoken almost exclusively in the Global North. In contrast, Wikipedia editions written in languages common to the Global South were smaller and much less developed, even if the language in question was widely spoken:

Table 6.3. Most Widely Spoken Languages (2019)

Language	Articles (of 33.1 million)	Percentage of All Wikipedia Articles	Percentage of World Speaks That Language
Mandarin	0.88 million	2.66%	14.51%
Hindi	0.12 million	0.36%	8.00%
Standard Arabic	0.46 million	1.39%	3.55%
Bengali	0.06 million	0.18%	3.45%
Indonesian	0.33 million	1.00%	2.59%

Sources: Wikimedia Foundation, "Wikipedia Statistics"; *Ethnologue*, "What Are the Top 200 Most Spoken Languages?" 2019, archived at https://w.wiki5Bh3; and World Bank, "Population, Total" [2019], https://data.wowrldbank.org/indicator/SP.POP.TOTL.

Now, admittedly, these numbers are somewhat fuzzy and far from concrete, but they nevertheless suggest that languages common to the Global North are likely to be overrepresented across the many Wikipedia variants, whereas languages common to the Global South are likely to be underrepresented.

A second way that the Global North bias can be brought into view is by looking at article coverage regarding geography. In a 2013 report, the Oxford Internet Institute (OII) showed that out of 3.79 million geotagged articles selected from all the Wikipedia versions, "all of Africa combined contains only 2.6% of the planet's Wikipedia articles despite having 14% of the world's population and 20% of the world's land."[22] A subsequent OII report published in 2018 built on these findings by revealing that of 3.34 million geotagged articles selected from forty-four of the largest Wikipedias, articles geotagged to Western Europe numbered "slightly more than half of the global total" despite that portion of the world "occupying only about 2.5% of the world's land area."[23]

What causes this sort of preferentiality? One obvious answer is that—thanks to technology, infrastructure, education, and access—the Global North is simply where most editors come from, and people are more likely to write about the places they know. A 2018 survey of the broad Wikimedia community supports this hypothesis by revealing that 81.1 percent of all contributors were from the Global North, with 58.3 percent hailing from Europe[24] and 5.4 percent from North America; Africa's contributors, by comparison, made up 0.7 percent of the total, followed closely by Oceania's 0.8 percent share.[25]

To complicate matters, OII research suggests that whereas people from the Global North seem likely to write about the slice of the world that they are familiar with, people from the Global South are more likely to write about the Global North, too.[26] "Rather than editing an article about a local town or village, someone from a low-income country would be more likely to edit an article about New York or Paris," Mark Graham of the OII explained to *Wired* in a 2015 writeup.[27] Graham and his coauthors attribute this "pull" to "informational magnetism . . . cast by the world's economic cores";[28] this "magnetism" is nothing more than the cultural hegemony of the Global North, which "pulls" editors from across the globe toward it. This means that an additional challenge that Wikipedia faces is whether it can attract editors from the Global South who are also interested in writing about their often-marginalized parts of the world.

RACIAL BIAS

In 2020, the Wikimedia Foundation conducted a community survey that helped determine, among other things, the racial demographics of their many participants. The results showed that, when it comes to editors hailing from the United States, white/Caucasian participants are overrepresented, whereas black, Hispanic, or indigenous participants are underrepresented. The results looking at the United Kingdom were largely the same: white/Caucasian editors were overrepresented, whereas Asian and black participants were underrepresented.[29] These results—especially when considered alongside the experiences of many editors of color[30]—suggest that Wikipedia and its sister sites[31] have a definite racial bias. As with all issues discussed in this chapter, the exact reasons for this are unclear.

Jay Cassano of Fast Company suggests that it might be an indirect result of the underrepresentation of people of color in the technology sector.[32] (In the

United States, for instance, a 2017 report published by the Brookings Institution revealed that whereas black and Hispanic people make up 11.9 percent and 16.7 percent of the total workforce, respectively, these groups make up just 7.9 percent and 6.8 percent of the tech field itself.)[33] Because people in the tech field are often more likely to contribute to the site, a demographic imbalance in this domain could result in lopsided editor numbers.[34]

Another hypothesis has to do with internet access. According to a 2021 survey by the Pew Research Center that looked at in-home broadband access in the United States, 80 percent of white adults confirmed that they had broadband in their house, but only 71 percent of black adults and 65 percent of Hispanic adults said the same.[35] If fewer people of color have direct access to the internet, then it makes sense that fewer of them would be able to contribute to the site.

Either way, the overrepresentation of white editors has caused noticeable problems with topical coverage. This is because white editors, as members of a systemically privileged racial group in modern society, are more likely to create or edit articles that magnify white voices like their own. Articles about people of color, in contrast, are often neglected (or simply are not created). When readers see these underdeveloped articles, they unconsciously assume that white individuals are more "notable" than persons of color, which in turn helps uphold the extant systems of white supremacy embedded in many (especially Western) cultures. Now, this does not mean that all white editors are evil people who go out of their way to produce overtly racist content. Instead, this is evidence of systemic racism, which is insidious and often perpetuated in small, sometimes unconscious ways. But however small or unconscious those acts may be, they still have a real-world impact that perpetuates inequality.

As with the gender imbalance, Wikipedia's racial bias has encouraged editors to band together to improve the site's coverage. One of the first of these projects to form was the "Black Lunch Table" (BLT) venture, an initiative founded in 2005 by Jina Valentine (an assistant professor of print media at School of the Art Institute of Chicago) and Heather Hart (a visual artist based out of New York City). The two formed the project to document oral history about black visual art, as well as create Wikipedia articles about key black visual artists.[36] The project has been a smash success, and in 2020 alone, it helped 342 editors create 146 new articles.[37]

Another project in this vein is AfroCROWD initiative, started by Haitian lawyer Alice Backer in 2015. This project aims to increase coverage of African topics and encourage Africans (as well as people of African descent) to become active contributors. Like BLT, AfroCROWD has organized edit-a-thons and helped create hundreds of articles about racially marginalized people. (AfroCROWD also oversees the AfricaCROWD, HaitiCROWD, and AfroLatino-CROWD projects, which aim to improve coverage of African, Haitian, and Afro-Latino topics, respectively.) Taking one glance at the articles that AfroCROWD and the Black Lunch Table have created is more than enough to recognize their impact. But as with all things, work is still to be done, and as I write this sentence, many nonwhite ethnic groups still lack editor representation and topical coverage on Wikipedia.

OTHER BIASES OF NOTE

Although the three biases that I just discussed are among the biggest to plague the site, they are far from the only ones causing problems. One bias that does not get as much airtime, so to speak, is the issue of "recentism." Wikipedia defines this as a phenomenon wherein "an article has an inflated or imbalanced focus on recent events."[38] To better understand this, imagine an article about a country that has been around for five hundred years. Now imagine that this article's "Historical development" section focuses almost entirely on the country's past few decades at the expense of everything else. This would be an example of recentism.

This bias is often a simple result of the way Wikipedia works: thanks to the site's "high-tempo and decentralized editing process,"[39] information can be added to the site as soon as it's released. This encourages an implicit bias toward contemporaneous sourcing, as these sources are often the most plentiful and easiest to find (especially in the digital realm). Another reason for recentism is that older sources, which might provide better historical coverage of a topic, are often in harder-to-access places; if an editor wants to access old newspapers from the 1800s, for instance, they might have to go through a paywall, or physically track down microfiche from their local library.

Another bias that has impacted Wikipedia's coverage is the widespread (and sometimes exclusive) use of online sources as references, which skews coverage to only what can be found online. The reason for this bias is simple: thanks to the speed and connectivity of the internet, people have a much easier time locating online sources than they do offline sources. Of course, reliable and easy-to-access Web resources—such as open-access articles or reputable Web portals—are perfectly acceptable as Wikipedia references, but editors should be cautious about *only* using online sources. After all, much of the world's strongest research is still published in journals and books locked behind paywalls or shelved in libraries. For editors who have access to these offline resources (e.g., students, professors, archivists), the challenge thus becomes, as one Wikipedian colorfully put it, "getting away from the screen and [going] into a library"[40] to find your sources.

The final type of bias that I want to discuss is one that I myself am guilty of perpetuating: the pop culture bias. I use this catch-all phrase to refer to the fact that although Wikipedia is supposed to cover all human knowledge, a disproportionate number of articles focus on contemporary pop culture. Johnny Au, for instance, once bemoaned that "more has been written about [the television series] *The Simpsons* . . . than about all of John Milton's works (including *Paradise Lost*) *combined*" [emphasis in original].[41]

Other examples are plentiful: In early 2022, for instance, the article on the fictional superhero Batman (composed of 21,833 words) was bigger than the article about Bats (16,998 words), and the article for Steven Spielberg's 1981 film *Raiders of the Lost Ark* (17,974 words) was more than twice the length of the article on the actual Ark of the Covenant (7,412 words). The proverbial cherry on top is that, of the pop culture articles the site features, a large number focus on media produced by privileged groups of people (e.g., men, white people, Americans)—which clearly illustrates the interwovenness of the other biases that I have talked about in this section.[42]

A SYSTEMIC BARRIER

The biases discussed so far in this chapter have emerged and metastasized for different reasons, but on some level, they are all enabled by a key element of Wikipedia's approach to knowledge organization: the mandate that articles be neutral and eschew "original research" in favor of what reliable, verifiable sources have to say. This policy is arguably a double-edged sword. On one hand, it helps prevent articles from filling up with unsourced nonsense.[43] But on the other, it means that editors must use material that has already been published—and this material, regardless of its "authoritativeness," is often far from neutral or objective. Consider, for instance, the myriad history books that excluded or minimized the contributions of women and people of color. Or the scholarship from or about the Global South, which is still often overshadowed by material produced by or focusing on the Global North. And then there are cultures that lack verifiable records, or whose records were destroyed by the genocidal flames of colonialism. Because the cultural knowledge of these societies cannot be substantiated through conventional means, that knowledge cannot be added to Wikipedia.[44]

The sad truth is that, despite what many academics tell themselves, the body of information that we call "reliable" scholarship is full of holes and laced with various stripes of bias. Unfortunately, it is this scholarship—warts and all—that Wikipedia editors must rely on when editing the site, meaning that Wikipedia articles will logically reflect the biases of their sources. (The problem is made all the worse when you realize that Wikipedia, as one of the most popular sites online, could very easily beam biased content to millions of readers.) The site's seeming impotence in the face of source bias is perhaps Wikipedia's biggest flaw, and short of infrastructural reform, topical imbalance and lopsided editor demographics will continue to be a problem. But although it might be impossible to completely "fix" Wikipedia within its existing framework,[45] contributors can use certain practices to mitigate much of the damage that source and editor bias causes.

BECOMING A "CRITICAL EDITOR"

The question of how one can detect and "revert" the biases embedded in the core of Wikipedia is an important one to ask, and it arguably calls for a new way of contributing that I like to call *critical editing*.[46] This approach is a subset of critical pedagogy and can be glossed as a holistic set of tactics that recognize Wikipedia not as the neutral "sum of all human knowledge," but as a political nexus of ever-changing knowledge (re)production; this means that calls for neutrality are usually just calls for the status quo. Critical editors also accept as self-evident that power dynamics are inherent in supposedly "reliable" sources as well as the encyclopedic project itself; the only way to fight these asymmetries is by rigorously scrutinizing articles for unconscious slant, systematically interrogating our existing citational practices, and dialoging with other editors about ways to improve the site's coverage.

Critical editing is not a magical panacea that will erase all bias, but when embraced consistently and committedly, it has the potential to make Wikipedia a more balanced site that reflects the knowledge of the world. Implicit in this approach are four key features, which have been based on educator Ira Shor's understanding of critical consciousness: power awareness, critical literacy, desocialization, and self-organization/self-education.

Criterion 1: Power Awareness

Arguably the foundational aspect of critical editing is the awareness of *power*, who wields it, and how it is structured. On Wikipedia, power often manifests itself through practices of sourcing. After all, the site, you will remember, is epistemologically citational, meaning that its articles are based on what "reliable sources" have to say; if a topic lacks "reliable sources," then that topic will not receive an article. The problem here is that, per the way Wikipedia defines them, "reliable sources" are almost always the product of Western publishers or commercial media companies. By producing sources that are deemed reliable, these publishers have an indirect say in determining what can and cannot be added to the site. For this reason, massive publishers have power in shaping Wikipedia's content.

Power awareness should also be a reflexive act; after all, critical editors are in a position of power, too, given that Wikipedia is very literally "made and remade by" their editing choices.[47] Because editors determine the size and scope of the site, and because Wikipedia is often treated by its global readership as the end-all-be-all "sum of human knowledge," any topical omission on the site will likely result in snowballing ignorance about that topic. By strategically choosing which articles to (not) create or (not) edit, an editor could control in a very real sense the way the world thinks about any given topic. It is imperative for critical editors to recognize the power that their position grants and the responsibility that they bear.

Criterion 2: Critical Literacy

Second, critical editors should strive to be "critically literate." Ira Shor glosses "critical literacy" as the ability "to read and write as part of the process of becoming conscious of one's experience as historically constructed within specific power relations."[48] For a Wikipedia editor, this means eschewing shallow understandings of a text, be it a source or a completed article. Instead, editors should strive to recognize the many dimensions of a text by asking critical questions about it: Who wrote this work? Why did they write it? Who published it? Has it been discussed in the literature? If so, what have others said about it? Has it been critiqued? If so, why? Ultimately, the critical editor should recognize that "information resources reflect their creators' expertise and credibility"—as well as biases—and must therefore be "evaluated based on the information need and the context in which the information will be used."[49]

Critical literacy is a crucial skill for editors to learn, given that not all "reliable sources" are made equal: an opinion piece published in the *Wall Street Journal* advocating for lessened restrictions on oil drilling, for instance, is likely to have a different purpose than a peer-reviewed journal article published in *Science* warning about climate change, even though both would likely be seen on Wikipedia as acceptable "reliable sources." A critical editor should thus interrogate where a source is coming from, and, if necessary, question why the producers of that source were motivated to release it in the first place. In doing so, critical editors can discover whether sources are overly biased and whether their inclusion on Wikipedia will give undue weight to prejudiced ideas.

If you are interested in learning more about critical literacy, see Hilary Janks's book *Doing Critical Literacy: Texts and Activities for Students and Teachers* (2014), which includes several "models of practice" that can increase your critical skills, both as a Wikipedia editor and a student of life in general.

Criterion 3: Desocialization

Third, critical editors should strive to desocialize—or perhaps we could say "culturally deprogram"—themselves, thereby "recognizing and challenging" the problematic "myths, values, behaviors, and language learned in mass culture."[50] Now, this does not mean that we should dart into the woods and cut ourselves off from the decadence of the late capitalist hellscape we have found ourselves living in; it is simply the call to *think* about what we know and believe to be "true." This is important because so much of what we humans take as "common sense" is arbitrary, fallacious, or simple tradition wrapped in pseudofacts.

This desocialization should also include a critical look at rhetoric popular on Wikipedia. For instance, Wikipedia editors often assert that the site is neutral, because it catalogs only what other sources have said about a topic, but doesn't that system of citation show a bias toward a very specific style of sourcing? What about oral tradition? Likewise, Wikipedia boasts that it collects and transmits the "sum of all human knowledge" the world over, but aren't there important topics that Wikipedia barely mentions? The idea that Wikipedia is truly neutral or equal in its topical coverage is an example of the "myths, values, [and] behaviors" that critical editors should strive to rid themselves of.[51]

Desocialization, at its core, is fundamentally metacognitive—it is thinking about ways of thinking. In general, metacognition is often a difficult, taxing task, and in this case, it's made all the trickier by the fact that we are trying to identify ways of thinking that for many are deeply internalized, blending into the background of the mind. Sometimes, this sort of self-critique can feel like searching for a polar bear in a snowstorm. To aid in this task, I often recommend Mahzarin R. Banaji and Anthony G. Greenwald's book *Blindspot: Hidden Biases of Good People*, which lucidly explores the many ways otherwise decent people fail to recognize and question their innate biases and cultural assumptions. (Although Banaji and Greenwald never mention the term "desocialization," I would argue that it is nevertheless an ideal that drives much of their book.)

Criterion 4: Self-Organization and Self-Education

Finally, the critical editor "[takes] part in and [initiates] social change projects" divorced from "authoritarian relations."[52] Put in simpler language, this means that critical editors contribute content to the site not because they have to (such as a student who has been given a mandatory school assignment to "improve an article"), but because they *want* to. Only by breaking from the existing power structures—which, according to the famed Brazilian educator Paulo Freire, engender an "authoritarian and acritical frame of mind"[53]—and embracing self-direction can the critical editor strive for anything that resembles liberation. You could reasonably argue that self-organization and self-education are the criteria of critical editing with which most Wikipedians are already familiar, given that many of them contribute to the site for no reason other than for their own enjoyment or edification.

HOW TO READ AN ARTICLE CRITICALLY

With these four facets of critical editing in mind, I would now like to discuss how a critical editor might read a Wikipedia article, keeping an eye out for bias and other problematic content.

Step 1: Look Over the Article

The first step is to, quite simply, glance at the article in question; often, the "look" of a page can speak volumes about its quality. Is it divided into logical sections? Does the article's coverage seem reasonable? Are key words or phrases hyperlinked? Are there infoboxes or images to better present/illustrate information? Is the article sorted into categories? Does it have a section for external links or related articles? Conversely, what is the article missing? Does it lack content? Are huge chunks of text unsourced?

It is also worthwhile to look at the upper right-hand corner of the article. If you see a green circle or a gold star, that means that the page has been promoted to "good" or "featured" article status, respectively.[54] As discussed in chapter 4, a "good" article has been reviewed by another editor, and a "featured" article has been reviewed by a whole panel of editors. The "good" and "featured" article badges can, therefore, clue you in that the article in question has been unofficially peer-reviewed. *Caveat lector!* Just because an article seems to be free of bias does not mean it *is* unbiased (as they say, you should never judge a book solely by its cover). To determine the true quality of an article, you will need to review its content in detail.

Step 2: Read the Main Text

Turn to the article's prose. Is the writing understandable to a layperson? Does the text attempt to convey the subject matter in a relatively straightforward, impartial way, or is it rife with biased language? When looking for bias, it is especially useful to keep an eye out for "peacock terms," "weasel words," and unnecessary editorializing.

"Peacock terms" (also known as "puffery") are instances of loaded language that uncritically promotes an article's subject, akin to how a peacock shows off its feathers to woo a mate. "Paul Thomas is a talented Wikipedia editor and one of the world's greatest writers" is an example of a sentence blighted by needless *peacockery*, given that words such as "talented" and "greatest" unnecessarily skew the importance of the sentence's subject.[55]

"Weasel words" are terms or phrases that take an ambiguous, biased, or patently false assertion and through complex sophistry make it sound authoritative. Consider this example: "Some experts say that Paul Thomas is one of the world's best Wikipedia editors." On the surface, this sentence might seem objective, because it attributes a subjective claim (i.e., "Paul Thomas is one of the world's best Wikipedia editors") to a source (i.e., "Some experts"). The problem is that the source is vague to the point of meaninglessness; who are these "experts," exactly, and why should we listen to them? Often, weaselly sentences can be fixed with a simple rewrite (e.g., "Paul Thomas's mother thinks that Paul is one of the world's best Wikipedia editors"), but other times, these sentences will need to be excised wholesale.[56]

Finally, watch out for unnecessary editorializing, or instances in which an editor has gone beyond what a reference says and has instead given their own opinion about a topic. Examples include subjective or provocative labels (e.g., "Paul Thomas is an idiot"),[57] unsourced expressions of doubt (e.g., "This book is *supposedly* reliable"),[58] or words that inappropriately convey emphasis (e.g., *"It should be noted* that Paul Thomas is a writer").[59] All these writing flourishes skew, misread, or ignore the actual content of their sources and are thus a violation of Wikipedia's "no original research" policy.

Step 3: Check the Sourcing

If the article's prose seems solid, turn to its sourcing. Is every statement backed up with a citation, or is the text bereft of references? In the case of the latter, proceed with skepticism: Wikipedia is fundamentally citational, meaning that every claim on the site needs to have a source. A statement without a source is not easily verified and, therefore, could be false.[60] (Sometimes unsourced statements will be marked with the superscript [citation needed] tag.[61] Think of this tag like a warning sign, alerting you to potentially dubious information that has not yet been culled from the site.) It is also possible that a citationless claim is true but for whatever reason has yet to be sourced; if you know of a quality reference right off the bat that could back up an otherwise unsubstantiated claim, it never hurts to add it. But in all things, remember the adage: "Exceptional claims require exceptional sources."

If an article does contain references, you will then want to determine whether those sources are reliable or whether they are unnecessarily biased. To do this, ask yourself:

- Who wrote the source in question? Are those individuals qualified to write about the topic at hand? How so?
- What about the publishers? Were they motivated by money? Politics? Education?
- Was the reference peer-reviewed/fact-checked, or was it released by a group known for shoddy, sensationalist scholarship?
- How old is the source? Have newer works supplanted it? Are they used in the article, too?
- Does the article omit certain sources? Does this omission skew the article's coverage?

The glut of "fake news" that has proliferated in the past few years can make the analysis of sources a challenge, because many questionable sources can look legitimate on the surface. If you are unsure of the reliability of a source, feel free to visit the Wikipedia:Reliable sources/Noticeboard page and start a discussion; many seasoned editors frequent this portal, eagerly helping others determine whether a source is useful or should be quickly discarded.

Even if a work appears reliable, you still should not take what is on Wikipedia at face value; after all, a ne'er-do-well editor could have slapped a real source onto the end of an otherwise false statement and then added that to

Wikipedia. For this reason, it is always best practice to track down a source and confirm that it is being used appropriately on Wikipedia. (As an aside, going to the original source can also help people break the bad habit of relying exclusively on tertiary sources for research.) Sometimes you can access original sources online through portals such as Google Books or Archive.org; at other times, you might need to contact your local library for assistance.

Step 4: Look at the Article History

Pretend that you are reading a Wikipedia article, and it looks reliable: it might be nicely written, logically ordered, and thoroughly sourced. For all intents and purposes, the article seems solid. But how do you know the version you are looking at will be there tomorrow? What about in five minutes? What if the page has been persistently vandalized over the past few weeks, and you caught it at a good time? Or maybe the page has been at the center of a massive edit war, and editors have been flipping between two different versions of the article? A single look at the article is not sufficient to judge whether it is stable. The only way you can check for issues like this is by looking at an article's history page.

As was discussed in chapter 3, the history page logs every edit made to the page and stretches back to when the article was created. The history page also lists which editors have made which modifications, how big those edits were, and when the edits occurred. Most edits are accompanied by short edit summaries, which allow editors to detail the modifications they have made. Looking over a history page is an ideal way to determine an article's relative stability. Edit wars and recurrent bouts of vandalism, for instance, usually result in a history page that records the back-to-back addition and removal of similar content. A history page also allows you to contrast older revisions of an article with newer ones. This feature is quite useful if you are trying to track the modifications of a disruptive editor, or to revert misinformation that has been surreptitiously added into an article across several edits.

Step 5: Check the Talk Page

Another area that you should check is the article's talk page. Almost every talk page will feature a beige box at the top that indicates the WikiProject(s) into which the article has been sorted. This beige box will also indicate with a letter grade the article's quality; this is another useful feature to determine an article's worth "at a glance," but be aware that this grade can easily be changed by other editors. If the article in question has achieved "good" or "featured" status, the beige box will also contain a link to the reviews that led to the article being promoted.

Talk pages can also feature sections where editors discuss the content, layout, or scope of an article. Sometimes these discussions are relatively brief;

at other times, they are enormous, comprising dozens of comments posted over a long period of time. These conversation chains can often contextualize an article or help you pinpoint areas that might contain biased, problematic, or false information. If you believe that an article is substantially flawed, feel free to post on the article's talk page and start a dialogue with other editors.

HOW TO EDIT AN ARTICLE CRITICALLY

The other aspect of critical editing is, perhaps somewhat obviously, *editing*. If you are interested in improving the content of Wikipedia, this section outlines a few "best practices" and patterns of thinking that you might consider when contributing to the site. (Note that many of these suggestions are written in the imperative for purposes of grammatical simplicity; they are neither authoritative nor "compulsory." Critical editing by its very nature despises authoritarian mandates.)

Practices That Promote Power Awareness

First, keep in mind the issue of power and power relations. To hone your ability at identifying these often-invisible structures, consider working the following practices into your editing approach:

- When adding content to an article, ask yourself the following questions: Are the sources that I am using overwhelmingly the product of, for example, white men from the Global North? Do they represent a global perspective, or are they more focused on a Euro-American view of the topic? Do the sources exacerbate or ameliorate the site's gender or racial biases?
- Decolonize and/or diversify Wikipedia by citing marginalized, international, or indigenous scholars. This is especially important to consider if you are writing about a person from a marginalized group, or a culture group that is not your own.
- Be mindful of power dynamics when interacting with other editors, too. Thanks to their preponderance, white male editors from the Global North unofficially hold more power on the site; if you happen to be white, male, and/or from the Global North, meditate on the systemic power that you possess. Try to use it to magnify or center the efforts of marginalized editors.
- Reflect on your actions as an editor and question whether they uphold or dismantle the site's problematic power dynamics. Pay particular interest to the minor, "boring" details of your editing. For instance: How long do you spend editing the site on average? Do you own the reference material that you cite? From whose computer do you edit the site? These details can often speak volumes about your own position of power.

- Using the "History" tab of an article, see which user wrote most of that article's content. Look at that user's contributions to other pages. Do you notice problematic patterns of behavior? Do their edits show a consistent bias for or against certain sources?

Practices That Promote Critical Literacy

Second, critical editing requires a sense of critical literacy, or the ability to discern the origin, nature, and purpose of a text. To do this, you might:

- Read articles analytically, being mindful of what the text says as well as what it might imply. Could the text be misinterpreted? Is the text simply wrong? If so, how can the problem be addressed?
- Analyze an article's references, ensuring that not only are they accurate, but they have not been used to unfairly skew the article's contents. (When it comes to news outlets, a useful tool for determining bias is the "Media Bias Chart." This site, published by Ad Fontes Media at https://adfontes media.com/, tracks both the partisan bias of a new source and its relative accuracy.)
- If applicable, question whether the article relies too much on a single source when other sources might exist.
- Help fill out underdeveloped references by providing elements such as publisher information, date of access, identifying numbers, and so forth, so that others can more readily locate and analyze the source material.
- Excise overtly skewed references, especially if a reference exacerbates the site's bigger biases. If possible, replace these references with sources that push back against systemic bias and highlight marginalized voices. (A citation change might also require you to rewrite parts of an article.)
- If you discover a major error that cannot be fixed through simple edits, start an in-depth discussion about it on the Wikipedia:WikiProject Countering systemic bias talk page, or reach out to editors with whom you can thoroughly discuss—and ideally solve—the problem.
- When scrutinizing history pages, consider using a tool such as the "Who Wrote That?" extension (which enables you to see which editor added what string of text to any given article),[62] or the "WikiBlame" tool (which lets you search page revisions for keywords).[63]

Practices That Promote Desocialization

Third, critical editors need to crack through the ideology that has for so long blinded them to the "-isms" (e.g., sexism, racism) that plague both Wikipedia and society. Here are some methods to help you do this:

- Create or expand articles about underrepresented individuals, peoples, cultures, countries, languages, and so forth.
- Scan articles and edit out sexist language (e.g., "fireman" instead of "firefighter"), bigoted terms, or labels that unnecessarily define individuals by their gender, race, nationality, and so forth (e.g., "Jane Smith is a female writer").
- Remove or rewrite content that makes assumptions about the identity of the reader or about the way the world is "naturally" or "normally" structured.
- Consider contributing to a Wikipedia written in a language other than English; this can help fight against the normative assumption that the English Wikipedia is the "real" Wikipedia and that all other versions are just inferior reflections.
- Push back against the "regressive values operating" on Wikipedia,[64] such as guidelines that have played a structural role in preserving bias. Bring attention to the shortcomings of the NPOV and reliable source mandates by dialoging with other editors on talk pages.
- Emphasize that calls for "neutrality" can often be calls for nothing more than the status quo, which is far from "neutral."[65]
- Refrain from using language that paints Wikipedia as a utopia set apart from other human endeavors; instead, recognize that the site has problems that need to be addressed.
- Broadcast any coverage problems you may find, but also put effort into thinking of ways to fix those problems. (Giving criticism, after all, is often easier than solving the root problem.)
- If a reader or editor speaks up about possible bias on the site, take their concerns seriously and treat them with the respect they deserve. Tap into your empathy and start a dialogue with them. Brainstorm ways to fix the problem.

Practices That Promote Self-Organization and Self-Education

Finally, the critical editor embraces the ideals of self-organization and self-education to separate the creation and improvement of Wikipedia articles' from authoritarian power relations. To practice self-organization and self-education, consider these suggestions:

- Seek to contribute to Wikipedia for no reason other than to make it better, more comprehensive, and more inclusive.
- Avoid practices such as paid editing, which are not only entangled in "authoritarian relations" but can also get you in trouble.
- Change entrenched editing behaviors that further the site's biased coverage. You might do this by making a concerted effort to improve pages about

women, people with marginalized genders, topics about the Global South, or persons of color.
- Organize edit-a-thons to teach people (especially marginalized or under-represented people) how they, too, can contribute to Wikipedia.
- Talk to people "in real life" who are knowledgeable about certain topics and encourage them to become editors.
- Connect with new Wikipedia editors. Try to answer any questions they might have or offer your expertise. Encourage them to edit more, and help them if they find themselves in a sticky situation.
- Think of mistakes you make as learning experiences that will aid in future growth.
- Reach out to editors whom you trust and seek critical feedback about your articles or your editing practices solely for the purpose of self-improvement.

FINAL THOUGHTS OF A WOULD-BE CRITICAL EDITOR

Wikipedia's systemic bias is, for many editors, its dirty laundry, which for more than ten years has been the focus of Wiki-criticism. But despite increasing awareness of the problem, a sad truth is that bias remains a facet of the Wikipedia experience. This leaves editors like me at a crossroads: we can either ignore the bias, shrugging it off as just "the way it is going to be," or we can embrace editing practices that actively push back against lopsided coverage. As someone who believes in the egalitarian ideals that all knowledge is valuable and that everyone deserves to be heard, I am firmly committed to making the site better through critical editing practices. These practices—which I have outlined in this chapter—encourage editors to look out for potentially hidden power structures, practice critical literacy at every turn, desocialize themselves from oppressive "norms," and embrace self-organization and self-education. I recognize that Wikipedia, as the product of humans, will never be perfect, nor will any editor (including me) fully live up to all the ideals espoused in this chapter. That said, I truly do think that more attention to critical editing can at least make the site better. And in the end, isn't any reduction in systemic bias—big or small—ultimately worth it?

A Short Glossary of Wiki-Slang

#1lib1ref: A hashtag campaign that encourages librarians and other information professionals to add references to unsourced citations on Wikipedia. (1Lib1Ref)

Admin: Short for "administrator"; a Wikipedia user with the ability to perform certain tasks, such as deleting pages or protecting articles. (Wikipedia: Administrators)

AfD: Short for "Article for deletion"; refers to the digital space on Wikipedia where editors discuss whether selected articles should be deleted from the site. (Wikipedia:AFD)

Anon: See **Unregistered editor**.

Arbitration: A process, overseen by a panel of editors, enacted to end conduct disputes that other methods of conflict resolution have failed to settle. (Wikipedia:Arbitration)

Article: A page on Wikipedia, specifically used in reference to *encyclopedic* pages. (Wikipedia:What is an article?)

Ban: A formal prohibition, passed down by an admin (or an editor with similar privileges), that prevents an editor from modifying content on the site. Bans can be general or specific in scope, and they may be temporary. (Wikipedia:Banning policy)

Block: The technical method by which admins prevent disruptive editors or IP addresses from accessing and editing the site. (Wikipedia:Blocking policy)

BLP: Shorthand for "biographies of living persons"; often used to emphasize that any information about people currently living must be of the highest quality, both to avoid accusations of libel and to prevent Wikipedia from descending into tabloid journalism. (Wikipedia:Biographies of living persons)

Bluelink: See **Wikilink**.

Bot: An automated maintenance tool that functions like an editor, carrying out (usually otherwise tedious) operations such as mass page renaming. (Wikipedia:Bots)

Bureaucrat: A Wikipedia user with the ability to confer administrative privileges on editors, as well as revoke said privileges. (Wikipedia:Bureaucrats)

Category: A keyword used to group topically similar articles together; categories are listed on the bottom of articles in their footer space. (Help:Category)

CC: See **Creative Commons**.

Citation: See **Reference**.

Commons: See **Wikimedia Commons**.

Conflict of interest (COI): Editing Wikipedia in a way that benefits you or anyone with whom you have a relationship (e.g., friends, family) or financial connection. Conflicts of interest must be disclosed on Wikipedia, and editors must disclose whether and by whom they are being paid for their services. (Wikipedia:Conflict of interest)

Consensus: The outcome of an attempt to address the valid concerns of all editors involved in a discussion; consensus making is the process by which Wikipedia editors ideally cooperate with one another. (Wikipedia:Consensus)

Contributions: A list of all edits that a specific editor makes. (Help:User contributions)

Copyedit: A term used by Wikipedia editors to refer to edits ranging from proofreading all the way to more advanced syntax adjustments. (Wikipedia: Basic copyediting)

Copyright violation: The illegal or unauthorized use of copyrighted material on Wikipedia; this concept is related but not identical to plagiarism. (Wikipedia:Copyright violations)

Creative Commons: A nonprofit organization known for its "Creative Commons licenses" that allow otherwise copyrighted material to be used freely in certain cases. (Creative Commons)

Deletion: The process by which a Wikipedia page is removed from the site and no longer accessible by the public. (Wikipedia:Deletion policy)

Disambiguation: The process by which two or more articles with the same name are differentiated from one another; usually this is done by adding unique parentheticals to the titles of the articles in question. (Wikipedia: Disambiguation)

Edit conflict: An error that arises when two different editors make changes to the same article at the same time. This usually requires one of the editors to redo their edit(s). (Help:Edit conflict)

Edit summary: A short summary of changes made to an article that an editor can add before publishing said changes. (Help:Edit summary)

Edit war: An online conflict in which two or more editors repeatedly add content to an article while reverting the contributions that their opponent(s) made. Edit wars are disallowed on Wikipedia, as they can easily disrupt productive editing. (Wikipedia:Edit warring)

Edit-a-thon: An organized event wherein a group of people edit articles en masse, usually to improve Wikipedia's coverage of some specific topic. (Edit-a-thon)

Editor: An individual—registered or otherwise—who changes the content on Wikipedia. (Wikipedia:Wikipedians)

Essay: A Wikipedia article that is neither encyclopedic nor a policy page but, instead, lays out viewpoints or opinions generally accepted by the community at large, if unofficially. (Wikipedia:Essays)

External link: A hyperlink that leads off Wikipedia to a different (i.e., "external") site. (Wikipedia:External links)

Featured article: One of Wikipedia's best articles in terms of quality, as determined by a group of knowledgeable editors. (Wikipedia:FA)

GLAM: An acronym for "galleries, libraries, archives, and museums," often used in discussions about cultural heritage. (Wikipedia:GLAM)

Good article: An article that has been reviewed by one other editor and judged to be of quality. (Wikipedia:GA)

Good faith: The assumption that a potentially disruptive editor is well-intentioned but misguided, rather than actively malicious. Assuming good faith can help editors avoid unnecessary conflict. (Wikipedia:Assume good faith)

History: A component of a Wikipedia page (article or otherwise) that lists all changes made to that page. (Help:Page history)

Infobox: A box found in the top right-hand corner of an article that summarizes key information about the article in question. (Wikipedia:Manual of Style/Infoboxes)

IP editor: See **unregistered editor.**

Link: Short for a hyperlink, or a string of text leading from one Web page to another. Links can be "wikilinks" (i.e., links that connect one Wikipedia page to another) or "external links" (i.e., links that lead readers off Wikipedia to some other website). (Help:Link)

Link rot: An issue wherein the target page of a hyperlink moves to a new URL or goes offline altogether. (Wikipedia:Link rot).

Main namespace: The section of Wikipedia that contains encyclopedic information. (Wikipedia:Namespace)

Major edit: An edit that substantially adjusts, updates, or rearranges an article.

Mediation: A formal conflict resolution process in which a group of dedicated editors settle content disputes. (Wikipedia:Mediation)

MediaWiki: The software that enables Wikipedia to run. (MediaWiki)

Merge: The process whereby two (or more) Wikipedia articles are combined into one. (Wikipedia:Merging)

Minor editor: An edit that is small in scope and easy to miss; examples include fixing typos, adding/removing stray punctuation, or fixing broken links.

Move: The act of renaming an article. (Wikipedia:Moving a page)

Navbox: A collapsible template, usually found at the bottom of an article, that provides links to topically related articles. (Wikipedia:Navigation template)

Neutrality: Often abbreviated as "NPOV (an initialism for "neutral point of view"); this is a core policy of Wikipedia, mandating that all content on the site be devoid of editorial bias. (Wikipedia:Neutral point of view)

Original research: Unique, unpublished hypotheses, ideas, theories, or arguments found nowhere else; this material, lacking mention in the published literature, must not be included in Wikipedia articles. (Wikipedia:OR)

Peer review: A process in which one editor reviews an article, noting weaknesses and suggesting changes to make the article stronger. (Wikipedia:PR)

Pipe(d) link: A wikilink with display text that does not match the title of the destination article. (Wikipedia:Piped link)

Plagiarism: Reproducing content, either directly or exceptionally closely, without providing necessary credit, often via sourcing; this concept is related but not identical to copyright violation. (Wikipedia:Plagiarism)

Plain-text editor: See **Source editor**.

Protection: Restrictions placed on an article by an admin that prevent certain types of editors (e.g., unregistered editors) from modifying the contents of the article. (Wikipedia:Protection policy)

Public domain: Material no longer under copyright. This material can be freely copied into Wikipedia, but to avoid any accusations of plagiarism, you must provide a reference. (Wikipedia:Public domain)

Puffery: A form of original research manifesting as unnecessary, unreferenced adjectives that uncritically praise a topic. (Wikipedia:Wikipuffery)

Redlink: See **Wikilink**.

Redirect: An article that, when searched for, sends the reader to a differently named article. (Wikipedia:Redirect)

Reference: A source or citation that backs up facts in an article. Inline references appear as numbered, hyperlinked footnotes. These footnotes point the reader to the bottom of an article, where citations are given in full. (Help:Footnotes)

Registered editor: A Wikipedia editor who has signed up for a named account; these editors can create and move pages, unlike unregistered editors. (Wikipedia:User access levels)

Reliable source: A reference deemed acceptable by Wikipedia's editorial standards. A reliable source (sometimes abbreviated as "RS") is one generally released by a reputable publisher and/or written by a knowledgeable author. (Wikipedia:Reliable sources)

Renaming: The process by which an article's initial title is changed; this process is also referred to as "moving" a page. (Wikipedia:Moving a page)

Revert: Undoing a previous edit in whole, returning the page (i.e., "reverting") back to the way it looked originally. (Wikipedia:Reverting)

Rollback: An advanced variant of reverting wherein an editor returns an article back to an earlier state, undoing a string of edits along the way. (Wikipedia:Rollback)

Sandbox: A Wikipedia page that editors can freely edit to practice their skills or learn how certain features work. (Wikipedia:About the sandbox)

Section: A portion of an article, demarcated by a section heading. (Help:Section)

Sock puppet: A secondary account operated by an already registered Wikipedia editor that is used for unethical or deceitful reasons. (Wikipedia:Sockpuppetry)

Source: See **Reference**. "Source" (as in "source text") can also refer to the raw, unprocessed wikitext that the MediaWiki software reads to generate the final look of an article.

Source editor: The "traditional" edit window that allows an editor to modify an article by manipulating wikitext. (Help:Wikitext)

Stub: A short article in need of expansion. Stubs usually contain only the basic details of a given topic, lacking the robustness found (ideally) in other articles. (Wikipedia:Stub)

Systemic bias: Imbalance in Wikipedia's topical coverage caused by larger and more systemic institutional, cultural, and structural inequalities. Finding and reducing systemic bias should be a major goal of every editor. (Wikipedia:Systemic bias)

Talk page: A discussion portal connected to an article/user page, on which editors can discuss the content of the article/user page in question. Talk pages are accessed by going to a page on Wikipedia and choosing the "Talk" tab in the upper left-hand corner of the screen. (Help:Talk pages)

Task force: A subgroup of a larger WikiProject, focused on a very specific topic or task. (Wikipedia:WikiProject Council/Guide/Task forces)

Template: Elements on Wikipedia that can be embedded across a variety of pages, thereby reducing repetitive wikitext. (Wikipedia:Templates)

Unregistered editor: A person who edits without formally creating an account. These editors are largely anonymous, identified in edit history pages only by their IP addresses. (Wikipedia:IP)

User: See **Editor**.

User namespace: The section of Wikipedia dedicated to user pages and related talk pages. Pages belonging to this namespace feature the prefix *User*. (Wikipedia:Namespace)

User page: A Wikipedia page assigned to a registered editor; editors can use their user page's talk feature to communicate with one another. Editors often choose to include on their user page limited autobiographical information. (Wikipedia:User pages)

Vandalism: The malicious disruption of Wikipedia's primary purpose through the addition, deletion, or disturbance of encyclopedic text. Persistent vandalism can lead to bans or blocks. (Wikipedia:Vandalism)

Visual Editor: An alternative editing interface on Wikipedia that eschews the direct manipulation of wikitext; instead, it immediately and visually reflects any changes an editor makes to an article. (VisualEditor)

Watchlist: A customizable list that allows editors to keep track of certain articles; often used to prevent vandalism. (Help:Watchlist)

Weasel words: Ambiguous words/phrases that imply an assertion is more widely held than it really is. (Weasel word)

Wiki-markup: See **Wikitext**.

Wikilink: A link on Wikipedia that leads to another article or page. If the target page exists, the link will appear blue; if the target page does not exist, the link will be red. (H:WIKILINK)

Wikimedia Commons: An affiliate site of Wikipedia that hosts freely licensed media such as images and video. (Wikimedia Commons)

Wikimedia Foundation: The nonprofit organization founded by Jimmy Wales that owns and operates Wikipedia and its affiliate sites. (Wikimedia Foundation)

WikiProject: An organized group of Wikipedia editors that aims to achieve a specific goal via coordinated editing. (WikiProject)

Wikitext: The markup language that the MediaWiki software used to generate the final look of a page. Wikitext can be adjusted using the source editor. (Help:Wikitext)

Image Attribution

All images used in this book were taken from Wikipedia (https://en.wikipedia.org) and are available for free reuse, provided proper attribution, per https://en.wikipedia.org/wiki/Wikipedia:Copyrights. Credit for the images is as follows:

- Figures 3.1 and 4.7 taken from the article "Vampire bat" (https://en.wikipedia.org/wiki/Vampire_bat)
- Figures 3.4, 3.11, and 4.11 taken from the article "Little brown bat" (https://en.wikipedia.org/wiki/Little_brown_bat)
- Figures 3.5–3.10 and 3.12–3.13 taken from the article "North Island brown kiwi" (https://en.wikipedia.org/wiki/North_Island_brown_kiwi)
- Figure 3.16 taken from the article "Banana" (https://en.wikipedia.org/wiki/Banana)
- Figure 4.8 taken from the page "Wikipedia:Peer Review" (https://en.wikipedia.org/wiki/Wikipedia:Peer_review)
- Figure 4.9 taken from the article "Eastern red bat" (https://en.wikipedia.org/wiki/Eastern_red_bat)
- Figure 4.10 taken from the page "Wikipedia:Good article nominations" (https://en.wikipedia.org/wiki/Wikipedia:Good_article_nominations)
- Figures 4.12–4.13 taken from the page "Wikipedia:Featured article candidates" (https://en.wikipedia.org/wiki/Wikipedia:Featured_article_candidates)
- Figures 3.2–3.3, 3.14–3.15, and 4.1–4.16 created using Wikipedia's Sandbox tool (https://en.wikipedia.org/wiki/Wikipedia:Sandbox)

All images used in this book are licensed for reuse through the Creative Commons Attribution-ShareAlike 3.0 Unported License and the GNU Free Documentation License.

Notes

INTRODUCTION

1. wiktionary:Wikipedia#Verb.
2. The answer is 1990.
3. No, she didn't. (If you thought otherwise, you might be thinking of 1999's *Resident Evil 3: Nemesis*—a right classic, if you ask me.)
4. Wikipedia succinctly describes primary sources as "original materials that are close to an event, and are often accounts written by people who are directly involved" Wikipedia:PRIMARY.
5. Wikipedia defines these as sources that offer "an author's own thinking based on primary sources, generally at least one step removed from an event" Wikipedia:SECONDARY.
6. Wiki.

CHAPTER 1

1. Stephen Barney, W. J. Lewis, J. A. Beach, and Oliver Berghof, *The Etymologies of Isidore of Seville* (Cambridge, UK: Cambridge University Press, 2006), 11.
2. Andrew Brown, *A Brief History of Encyclopedias* (London, UK: Hesperus, 2011), 15-19; Robert Collison, *Encyclopaedias: Their History throughout the Ages* (New York: Hafner, 1964), 23-25.
3. Pliny the Elder, *Naturalis Historia*, preface.
4. Aude Doody, "Finding Facts in Pliny's Encyclopaedia: The Summarium of the *Natural History*," *Ramus* 30, no. 1 (2001): 1-22.
5. Collison, *Encyclopaedias*, 26.
6. Barney et al., *The Etymologies of Isidore of Seville*.
7. Barney et al., *The Etymologies of Isidore of Seville*, 24-25.
8. Brown, *A Brief History of Encyclopedias*, 63-74.
9. Ian Richard Netton, *Muslim Neoplatonists: An Introduction to the Thought of the Brethren of Purity* (London, UK: Routledge, 2002), 1.
10. David R. Knechtges, "Huang lan 皇覽 (Imperial Conspectus)," 400, and Harriet T. Zurndorfer, "The Passion to Collect, Select, and Protect: Fifteen Hundred Years of the Chinese Encyclopedia," 500, in *Encyclopaedism from Antiquity to the Renaissance*, ed. Jason König and Greg Woolf (Cambridge, UK: Cambridge University Press, 2013).
11. Zurndorfer, "The Passion to Collect, Select, and Protect," 514-15; Michael Dillon, *Encyclopedia of Chinese History* (London, UK: Routledge, 2016), 797-98.
12. *Enkuklios* means "circular" and *paideia* means "education."

13. Ann Blair, "Revisiting Renaissance Encyclopaedism," in *Encyclopaedism from Antiquity to the Renaissance*, ed. Jason König and Greg Woolf (Cambridge, UK: Cambridge University Press, 2013), 379–80; Elias Muhanna, *The World in a Book* (Princeton, NJ: Princeton University Press, 2019), 10.
14. Blair, "Revisiting Renaissance Encyclopaedism," 391–92.
15. Johann Heinrich Alsted, *Encyclopaedia septem tomis distincta*, "Tabulae Numero Triginta Octo."
16. Collison, *Encyclopaedias*, 124–25.
17. *Encycloaedia Britannica*, s.v. "Encyclopaedia Britannica," accessed June 10, 2021, https://www.britannica.com/topic/Encyclopaedia-Britannica-English-language -reference-work.
18. H. G. Wells, *World Brain* (Garden City, NY: Doubleday, 1938), 3–38, 83.
19. Wells, *World Brain*, 85.
20. Wells, *World Brain*, 87.
21. Zalta helped create the *Stanford Encyclopedia of Philosophy* in 1995.
22. Eric M. Hammer and Edward N. Zalta, "A Solution to the Problem of Updating Encyclopedias," *Computers and the Humanities* 31, no. 1 (1997): 47.
23. Joseph Reagle, "Good Faith Collaboration: The Culture of Wikipedia," in *History and Foundations of Information Science*, eds. Michael Buckland and Jonathan Furner, 32–35 (Cambridge, MA: MIT Press, 2010).
24. Larry Sanger, "The Early History of Nupedia and Wikipedia: A Memoir," in *Open Sources 2.0: The Continuing Evolution*, eds. Chris DiBona, Danese Cooper, and Mark Stone" 311 (Beijing, China: O'Reilly, 2006).
25. *Encyclopedia of Alabama*, s.v. "Jimmy Wales," accessed June 14, 2021, http://www .encyclopediaofalabama.org/article/h-2618.
26. Katherine Mangu-Ward, "Wikipedia and Beyond: Jimmy Wales' Sprawling Vision," *Reason*, 2007, https://web.archive.org/web/20070814001555/https://reason .com/news/show/119689.html.
27. Marshall Poe, "The Hive," *The Atlantic*, 2006. https://www.theatlantic.com/ magazine/archive/2006/09/the-hive/305118/?single_page=true.
28. *Encyclopedia of Alabama*, s.v. "Jimmy Wales."
29. Andy Potts, "The Free-Knowledge Fundamentalist," *The Economist*, 2008, https:// www.economist.com/technology-quarterly/2008/06/07/the-free-knowledge -fundamentalist.
30. Andrew Lih, *Wikipedia Revolution: How a Bunch of Nobodies Created the World's Greatest Encyclopedia* (New York: Hyperion, 2009), 32.
31. Sanger, "Early History of Nupedia and Wikipedia," 313.
32. Lih, *Wikipedia Revolution*, 33.
33. Sanger, "Early History of Nupedia and Wikipedia," 312.
34. Lih, *Wikipedia Revolution*, 35; Jared Duval, *Next Generation Democracy* (New York: Bloomsbury, 2010), 75.
35. Sanger, "Early History of Nupedia and Wikipedia," 312.
36. Sanger, "Early History of Nupedia and Wikipedia," 313.
37. Sanger, "Early History of Nupedia and Wikipedia."
38. Nupedia Review Board, "Nupedia.com Editorial Policy Guidelines," archived June 7, 2001, http://web.archive.org/web/20010607080354/www.nupedia.com/policy .shtml#approvalov.

39. See https://hybridpedagogy.org/about/.
40. Nupedia editors, "Nupedia: Newest Articles," archived December 4, 2000.
41. Nupedia editors, "Nupedia: Newest Articles," archived December 5, 2001.
42. Sanger, "Early History of Nupedia and Wikipedia," 315.
43. Jason Mittell, "Wikis and Participatory Fandom," in *The Participatory Cultures Handbook*, ed. Aaron Delwiche and Jennifer Jacobs Henderson, 35 (New York: Routledge, 2013).
44. Ward Cunningham and Bo Leuf, *The Wiki Way: Quick Collaboration on the Web* (Boston: Addison-Wesley, 2001), 15, 17.
45. Dariusz Jemielniak, *Common Knowledge? An Ethnography of Wikipedia* (Stanford, CA: Stanford University Press, 2014), 10.
46. Cunningham and Leuf, *The Wiki Way*, 16–17.
47. RationalWiki, accessed June 22, 2021, https://rationalwiki.org/wiki/Rational Wiki:Technical_support.
48. Ballotpedia, accessed June 22, 2021, https://ballotpedia.org/MediaWiki.
49. Fandom, accessed June 22, 2021, https://community.fandom.com/wiki/Help: MediaWiki.
50. Sanger, "Early History of Nupedia and Wikipedia," 315–16.
51. Larry Sanger, quoted in Reagle, "Good Faith Collaboration, "39. The original emphasis used all caps.
52. Ruth Ifcher, e-mail message to Nupedia listserv, January 10, 2001, archived at http://web.archive.org/web/20030503010754/http://www.nupedia.com/ pipermail/nupedia-l/2001-January/000677.html.
53. Michael Kulikowski, e-mail message to Nupedia listserv, January 10, 2001, archived at http://www.logicmuseum.com/x/index.php?title=Wikipedia_origin_(Timeline).
54. Carl Anderson, e-mail message to Nupedia listserv, January 12, 2001, archived at http://www.logicmuseum.com/x/index.php?title=Wikipedia_origin_(Timeline).
55. Sanger, "Early History of Nupedia and Wikipedia," 317.
56. Sanger, "Early History of Nupedia and Wikipedia."
57. https://en.wikipedia.org/w/index.php?oldid=908493298.
58. Early Wikipedia articles were written using camel case (e.g., "camelCase," rather than "camel case").
59. "Wikimedia Statistics," Wikimedia Foundation, accessed June 22, 2021, https:// stats.wikimedia.org/#/en.wikipedia.org/content/pages-to-date/normal|table |2001-01-01~2002-05-01|page_type~content|monthly.
60. Sanger, "Early History of Nupedia and Wikipedia," 324.
61. Sanger "Early History of Nupedia and Wikipedia," 318.
62. Lih, *Wikipedia Revolution*, 136.
63. Wikimedia Foundation.
64. Wikipedia:Wikipedia Signpost/2005-07-25/Market share report.
65. Wikipedia:Wikipedia Signpost/2005-07-25/Market share report.
66. History of Wikipedia.
67. John Seigenthaler, "A False Wikipedia 'Biography,'" *USA Today*, 2005. http://usa today30.usatoday.com/news/opinion/editorials/2005-11-29-wikipedia-edit_x.htm.
68. Chloe Stothart, "Web Threatens Learning Ethos," *The Times Higher Education Supplement*, 2012, https://www.timeshighereducation.co.uk/story.asp?sectioncode =26&storycode=209408.

69. Jim Giles, "Internet Encyclopaedias Go Head to Head," *Nature* 438, no. 7070 (2005): 900, https://doi.org/10.1038/438900a.
70. Barry X. Miller, Karl Helicher, and Teresa Berry, "I Want My Wikipedia!" *Library Journal*, 2007, https://www.libraryjournal.com/?detailStory=i-want-my-wikipedia.
71. Adam R. Brown, "Wikipedia as a Data Source for Political Scientists: Accuracy and Completeness of Coverage," *PS: Political Science & Politics* 44, no. 2 (2011): 339–43, doi:10.1017/S1049096511000199.
72. Jona Kräenbring, Tika Monzon Penza, Joanna Gutmann, Susanne Muehlich, Oliver Zolk, Leszek Wojnowski, Renke Maas, Stefan Engelhardt, and Antonio Sarikas, "Accuracy and Completeness of Drug Information in Wikipedia: A Comparison with Standard Textbooks of Pharmacology," *PLOS One* 9, no. 9 (2014): 1, https://doi.org/10.1371/journal.pone.0106930.
73. Special:Statistics (as of December 25, 2021).
74. Special:Statistics.
75. "Siteviews Analysis," Toolforge, accessed January 3, 2022, https://pageviews.toolforge.org/siteviews/?platform=all-access&source=pageviews&agent=user&range=last-year&sites=en.wikipedia.org.
76. "Top Sites," Alexa Internet, accessed December 25, 2021, https://www.alexa.com/topsites.
77. Wikipedia:Size_in_volumes (as of December 25, 2021).

CHAPTER 2

1. Wikipedia:Five pillars. I have modified the second pillar slightly, changing it from "Wikipedia is written from a neutral point of view" to "Wikipedia's Content Is Neutral, Citational, and Never Original."
2. Wikipedia:ENC.
3. For those interested in contributing to an open-source dictionary, consider visiting Wiktionary (https://www.wiktionary.org/), which is Wikipedia's sister site dedicated to the creation of a multi-language word repository.
4. Wikipedia:FALSEBALANCE.
5. P. L. Thomas, "Power, Responsibility, and the White Men of Academia." Huffington Post, 2017, https://www.huffpost.com/entry/power-responsibility-and-the-white-men-of-academia_b_592d58bce4b08861ed0ccbce.
6. For more on this, see Zachary J. McDowell and Matthew A. Vetter, *Wikipedia and the Representation of Reality* (London, UK: Routledge, 2022).
7. Wikipedians often rebut critics of the NPOV by pointing out that the mandate governs the behavior of editors, not the site's content Wikipedia:NEUTRALEDIT. This rebuttal, however, still leaves open the potential for bias. For more on this, see McDowell and Vetter (in particular, 5–7).
8. Wikipedia:QUESTIONABLE.
9. Wikipedia:OR.
10. Amy Chozick, "Jimmy Wales Is Not an Internet Billionaire," *New York Times*, 2013, https://www.nytimes.com/2013/06/30/magazine/jimmy-wales-is-not-an-internet-billionaire.html.

11. Rose Eveleth, "How Much Is Wikipedia Worth?," *Smithsonian Magazine*, October 7, 2013, https://www.smithsonianmag.com/smart-news/how-much-is-wikipedia-worth-704865/.

12. Technically, content on the site is dual-licensed through both CC BY-SA 3.0 and the GNU Free Documentation License (GFDL) v. 1.3. Wikipedia previously published exclusively under the GFDL v. 1.2 license before moving to CC BY-SA 3.0 in 2009. According to Wikimedia, "CC-BY-SA [is] the primary Wikimedia license for text, and GFDL [is] a secondary license" (see meta:Licensing update/Implementation). For this reason, the present section focuses only on CC BY-SA.

13. This URL can lead to the Wikipedia article itself, or a "stable online copy that is freely accessible, which conforms with the license, and which provides credit to the authors in a manner equivalent to the credit given on the Project website." For more, see foundation:Terms of Use.

14. Creative Commons Australia, *Attributing Creative Commons Materials* (Brisbane, Australia: Australian Research Council Centre of Excellence for Creative Industries and Innovation; Creative Commons Australia, 2008), 7.

15. Wikipedia:No personal attacks.

16. strategy:Former Contributors Survey Results.

17. Emma Paling, "Wikipedia's Hostility to Women," *The Atlantic*, October 21, 2015, https://www.theatlantic.com/technology/archive/2015/10/how-wikipedia-is-hostile-to-women/411619/.

18. John Suler, "The Online Disinhibition Effect," *CyberPsychology & Behavior* 7, no. 3 (2004): 321–26, https://doi.org/10.1089/1094931041291295.

19. Alan Kirby, *Digitmodernism: How New Technologies Dismantle the Postmodern and Reconfig. Our Culture* (New York: Continuum, 2009), 114.

20. Robert Cummings and Matthew Barton, *Wiki Writing: Collaborative Learning in the College Classroom* (Ann Arbor: University of Michigan Press, 2008), 196.

21. Wikipedia:Ignore all rules.

22. Wikipedia:Consensus.

23. Wikipedia:NOTDEMOCRACY.

24. Wikipedia:Consensus.

25. Jemielniak, *Common Knowledge? An Ethnography of Wikipedia* (Stanford, CA: Stanford University Press, 2014), 62; Joseph Michael Reagle, "Good Faith Collaboration: The Culture of Wikipedia," in *History and Foundations of Information Science*, ed. Michael Buckland and Jonathan Furner, 14, 100, 107 (Cambridge, MA: MIT Press, 2010).

26. Tree Bressen, "Consensus Decision Making," in *The Change Handbook: The Definitive Resource on Today's Best Methods for Engaging Whole Systems*, ed. Peggy Holman, Tom Devane, and Steven Cady, 213 (San Francisco: Berrett-Koehler, 2007).

27. Felix Dodds, *Stakeholder Democracy: Represented Democracy in a Time of Fear* (London, UK: Routledge, 2019), 35.

28. Michael J. Sheeran, *Beyond Majority Rule: Voteless Decisions in the Religious Society of Friends* (Philadelphia, PA: Philadelphia Yearly Meeting of the Religious Society of Friends, 1983), 51.

29. Sheeran, *Beyond Majority Rule*.

30. On Wikipedia, the role is called an "admin"; Reagle, "Good Faith Collaboration," 107.

31. For Quakers, the role is called a "clerk"; Sheeran, *Beyond Majority Rule*, 51.
32. Wikipedia:No personal attacks; Sheeran, *Beyond Majority Rule*, 51, 53–62.
33. Dodds, *Stakeholder Democracy*, 35.
34. Sheeran, *Beyond Majority Rule*, 63; Wikipedia:Consensus.
35. Cf. the Quaker idea of "standing aside"; Dodds, *Stakeholder Democracy*, 36; Bressen, "Consensus Decision Making," 214.
36. For a laugh, see Wikipedia:Randy in Boise.
37. Wikipedia:There is no deadline. See also Wikipedia:Rome wasn't built in a day.
38. For more, see Wikipedia:Biographies of living persons.
39. Wikipedia:3RR.
40. Wikipedia:Arbitration.
41. Wikipedia:Conflict of interest.
42. Wikipedia:COIE.
43. Wikipedia:COVERT.
44. Taken from Wikipedia:Plagiarism.
45. Scott Greenberger, Rick Holbeck, John Steele, and Thomas Dyer, "Plagiarism Due to Misunderstanding: Online Instructor Perceptions," *Journal of the Scholarship of Teaching and Learning* 16, no. 6 (2016): 72–84; Michelle L. Zafron, "Good Intentions: Providing Students with Skills to Avoid Accidental Plagiarism," *Medical Reference Services Quarterly* 31, no. 2 (2012): 227.
46. In the spirit of attribution, this sentence uses names taken from Pendleton Ward's animated series *Adventure Time.*
47. Wikipedia:Ownership of content.
48. Wikipedia:STEWARDSHIP.
49. Wikipedia:Counter-Vandalism Unit/Vandalism studies/Study1.
50. For example, R. Stuart Geiger and Aaron Halfaker, "When the Levee Breaks: Without Bots, What Happens to Wikipedia's Quality Control Processes?," in *WikiSym '13: Proceedings of the 9th International Symposium on Open Collaboration*, 1–6 (New York: Association for Computing Machinery, 2013).

CHAPTER 3

1. Wikipedia:IP editors are human too.
2. All of the exceptions to this blanket statement are listed at Wikipedia:SOCKLEGIT.
3. For more on the misuse of multiple accounts, see Wikipedia:Sockpuppetry.
4. Wikipedia:Administrators.
5. Also accessible by searching Special:MyPage/sandbox.
6. The time is displayed using the Coordinated Universal Time standard, also known as UTC.
7. Wikidata; meta:WikiCite.
8. John Broughton, *Wikipedia: The Missing Manual* (Sebastopol, CA: O'Reilly, 2008), 17.
9. A more in-depth but highly technical discussion of templates can be found at Help:Template.

CHAPTER 4

1. This can be added by hitting Shift+\.
2. For more on this feature, see Wikipedia:Syntax highlighting, Syntax highlighting, and Help:Wikitext.
3. Wikipedia:Content assessment.
4. Wikipedia:Content assessment.
5. Wikipedia:Make technical articles understandable.
6. Wikipedia:FULL.
7. Wikipedia:Deletion policy#Speedy deletion.
8. Articles for deletion#Creating an AfD.
9. In 2019, this WikiProject was converted to a task force under the supervision of Wikipedia:TELEVISION.
10. Wikipedia:TASKFORCE.

CHAPTER 5

1. Amy Einsohn and Marilyn Schwartz, *The Copyeditor's Handbook: A Guide for Book Publishing and Corporate Communications*, 4th ed. (Oakland: University of California Press, 2019), 3.
2. See also LiAnna Davis, *Case Studies: How Professors Are Teaching with Wikipedia* (San Francisco: Wikimedia Foundation, 2012), http://education.wikimedia.org/casestudies, 5; LiAnna Davis, *Instructor Basics: How to Use Wikipedia as a Teaching Tool* (San Francisco: Wikimedia Foundation, 2012), http://education.wikimedia.org/instructorbasics, 4.
3. Wikipedia:Manual of Style.
4. MOS:LQ.
5. *Chicago Manual of Style*, 17th ed. (Chicago and London: University of Chicago Press, 2017), s.v. "6.9: Periods and Commas in Relation to Closing Quotation Marks."
6. *Chicago Manual of Style*; *New Oxford Style Manual* (Oxford, UK: Oxford University Press, 2016), s.v. "Quotation Marks."
7. Wikipedia:List of hoaxes on Wikipedia/Bicholim conflict.
8. See https://doaj.org/.
9. See http://oad.simmons.edu/oadwiki/Main_Page.
10. For more, see Wikipedia:The Wikipedia Library.
11. See also Davis, *Instructor Basics*, 9–10.
12. Although note that the different language editions of Wikipedia might have their own unique requirements about the translation process. See Wikipedia:Translate us.
13. Wikipedia:MACHINETRANSLATION. With that being said, MediaWiki has created a content creation tool that enables extended confirmed users to machine translate Wikipedia articles almost seamlessly from one language into another. Editors are discouraged from relying entirely on this tool, but it can give them a solid head start on translation projects. For more, see https://www.mediawiki.org/wiki/Content_translation.
14. Wikipedia:TFOLWP.
15. See also Davis, *Instructor Basics*, 11–13.

16. Due to the complexities of U.S. copyright law, there are exceptions. The statement here applies to most material published after January 1, 1926.
17. To add either a caption or a description in a different language, choose the option that reads "Add a caption/description in another language."
18. Katie Cunningham, *Accessibility Handbook: Making 508 Compliant Websites* (Beijing, China: O'Reilly, 2012), viii.
19. https://webaim.org/resources/contrastchecker/.
20. Jim Thatcher, Michael R. Burks, Christian Heilmann, et al., *Web Accessibility: Web Standards and Regulatory Compliance* (Berkeley, CA: Friends of ED, 2006), 4.
21. Sara Snyder, "Edit-a-thons and Beyond," in *Leveraging Wikipedia: Connecting Communities of Knowledge*, ed. Merrilee Proffitt, 123–25 (Chicago: ALA Editions, 2018). Wikipedia:EDITATHON#Clear goals.
22. Wikipedia:EDITATHON#Clear goals.
23. Wikipedia:EDITATHON#Determine logistics.
24. Snyder, "Edit-a-thons and Beyond," 128.
25. meta:Grants:Project/Rapid/Apply.
26. meta:Grants:Programs/Wikimedia_Community_Fund.
27. Wikipedia:WikiProject Mesoamerica.
28. Wikipedia:WikiProject Indigenous peoples of the Americas.
29. Wikipedia:Wikipedia Signpost/Newsroom/Suggestions.
30. Wikipedia:EDITATHON#Teach.
31. For example, Help:Cheatsheet.
32. Formerly Wikimetrics; https://eventmetrics.wmflabs.org/programs.
33. https://outreachdashboard.wmflabs.org/.
34. Andrew Lih, "What Are Galleries, Libraries, Archives, and Museums (GLAM) to the Wikimedia Community?," in *Leveraging Wikipedia: Connecting Communities of Knowledge*, ed. Merrilee Proffitt, 8–9 (Chicago: ALA Editions, 2018).
35. See Wikipedia:GLAM/Projects.
36. Lih, "What Are Galleries, Libraries, Archives, and Museums," 9, 14.
37. Wikipedia:GLAM/About.
38. Wikipedian in residence.
39. Institute of Museum and Library Services, "Government Doubles Official Estimate: There Are 35,000 Active Museums in the U.S." (Museum on Main Street Fact Sheet, May 19, 2014), https://www.imls.gov/news/government-doubles-official -estimate-there-are-35000-active-museums-us.
40. Institute of Museum and Library Services, *Public Libraries in the United States: Fiscal Year 2016* (Washington, DC: Institute of Museum and Library Services, 2018), vi, 2.
41. Jake Orlowitz, "The Wikipedia Library: The Largest Encyclopedia Needs a Digital Library and We Are Building It," in *Leveraging Wikipedia: Connecting Communities of Knowledge*, ed. Merrilee Proffitt, 80 (Chicago: ALA Editions, 2018).
42. https://citationhunt.toolforge.org/en?id=270afa5b.
43. As of January 2022, this tag is featured on 488,000 pages. See Template:Citation needed.
44. For a list of other online libraries, see List of digital library projects.
45. https://hashtags.wmflabs.org/?query=1lib1ref&project=en.wikipedia.org&start date=2016-01-01&enddate=2016-12-31&search_type=or&user=.

46. https://hashtags.wmflabs.org/?query=1lib1ref&project=en.wikipedia.org&start date=2021-01-01&enddate=2021-12-31&search_type=or&user=.
47. LiAnna Davis, *Case Studies*.
48. Outside the United States and Canada, many Wikimedia affiliates host similar programs. A list of available programs can be found at https://outreach.wikimedia .org/wiki/Education.
49. See https://dashboard.wikiedu.org/training/instructors/new-instructor-orientation.
50. LiAnna Davis, personal communication, November 16, 2021.
51. If you are working with Wiki Education, you will have access to a project Dashboard, through which you will be able to create the necessary number of accounts in one go.
52. Wiki Education has created a training module that helps instructors find articles for their students, which can be accessed at https://dashboard.wikiedu.org/training/ instructors/finding-articles.
53. Paul A. Thomas, M. F. Jones, and S. G. Mattingly. "Using Wikipedia to Teach Scholarly Peer Review: A Creative Approach to Open Pedagogy," *Journal of Information Literacy* 15, no. 2 (2021): 182–83, https://doi.org/10.11645/15.2.2913.

CHAPTER 6

1. Mark Graham, "Wikipedia's Known Unknowns," *The Guardian*, 2009, https://www .theguardian.com/technology/2009/dec/02/wikipedia-known-unknowns -geotagging-knowledge.
2. Ruediger Glott, Philipp Schmidt, and Rishab Ghosh, *Wikipedia Survey—Overview of Results—Overview of Results*, United Nations University and UNU-MERIT, 2010, http://www.wikipediastudy.org/docs/Wikipedia_Overview_15March2010-FINAL .pdf.
3. Wikimedia Foundation, *Wikipedia Editors Study Results from the Editor Survey*, April 2011 (San Francisco: Wikimedia Foundation, 2011), 3.
4. Wikimedia Foundation, *Community Engagement Insights 2018 Report* (San Francisco: Wikimedia Foundation, 2018).
5. Shyong K. Lam, Anuradha Uduwage, Zhenhua Dong, et al., "WP:Clubhouse? An Exploration of Wikipedia's Gender Imbalance," in *Proceedings of the 7th International Symposium on Wikis and Open Collaboration* (New York: Association for Computing Machinery, 2011), 7.
6. Joseph Reagle and Lauren Rhue, "Gender Bias in Wikipedia and Britannica," *International Journal of Communication*, 5 (2011): 1.
7. Jenny Singer, "The Women of Wikipedia Are Writing Themselves into History," *Glamour*, 2021, https://www.glamour.com/story/the-women-of-wikipedia-are -writing-themselves-into-history.
8. Tom Simonite, "The Decline of Wikipedia," *MIT Review* (2013).
9. Lam, Uduwage, Dong, et al., "WP:Clubhouse?," 6.
10. As to how the authors determine "notability," Claudia Wagner, Eduardo Graells-Garrido, David Garcia, and Filippo Menczer write, "We measure notability using the internal and external proxies based on language editions and search volume, respectively"; "Women through the Glass Ceiling: Gender Asymmetries in Wikipedia," *EPJ Data Science* 5, no. 5 (2016): 9.

11 Wagner, Graells-Garrido, Garcia, and Menczer, "Women through the Glass Ceiling."

12. Francesca Tripodi, "Ms. Categorized: Gender, Notability, and Inequality on Wikipedia," *New Media & Society* (2021): 10.

13. Wikipedia talk:WikiProject Women in Red/Archive 1#Scope.

14. Wikipedia talk:WikiProject Women in Red/Archive 1#Project name.

15. User:T Anthony/Women in Red.

16. Wikipedia:WikiProject Women in Red.

17. Robin Cembalest, "101 Women Artists Who Got Wikipedia Pages This Week," *ARTnews*, February 6, 2014, https://www.artnews.com/art-news/news/art-and-feminism-wikipedia-editathon-creates-pages-for-women-artists-2385/.

18. https://artandfeminism.org/about/.

19. *Oxford Reference*, s.v. "Global North," accessed August 17, 2021, https://doi.org/10.1093/acref/9780199599868.001.0001.

20. *Oxford Reference*, s.v. "Global South," accessed August 17, 2021, https://doi.org/10.1093/acref/9780191827822.001.0001.

21. Articles created by automated bots are not counted in these totals.

22. Ralph Straumann, Mark Graham, Bernie Hogan, and Ahmed Medhat, *Information Imbalance* (Oxford, UK: Oxford Internet Institute), https://www.ralphstraumann.ch/projects/information-imbalance-africa-on-wikipedia/.

23. Ralph Straumann and Mark Graham, *The Geographically Uneven Coverage of Wikipedia* (Oxford, UK: Oxford Internet Institute, 2014), https://www.oii.ox.ac.uk/news-events/news/the-geographically-uneven-coverage-of-wikipedia/.

24. Some 48.8 percent from Western Europe and 9.5 percent from Eastern Europe.

25. Wikimedia Foundation, *Community Engagement Insights 2018 Report*.

26. Mark Graham, Ralph K. Straumann, and Bernie Hogan, "Digital Divisions of Labor and Informational Magnetism: Mapping Participation in Wikipedia," *Annals of the Association of American Geographers* 105, no. 6 (2015): 1158–78.

27. James Temperton, "Wikipedia's World View Is Skewed by Rich, Western Voices," *Wired*, 2015, https://www.wired.co.uk/article/wikipedia-world-view-bias.

28. Graham, Straumann, and Hogan, "Digital Divisions of Labor and Informational Magnetism," 1158.

29. Wikimedia Foundation, *Community Insights/Community Insights 2021 Report*.

30. Wikipedia:Meetup/Black Lunch Table/online Aug2021; Samantha Melamed, "Edit-athon Aims to Put Left-Out Black Artists into Wikipedia," *Philadelphia Inquirer*, March 24, 2015, https://www.inquirer.com/philly/entertainment/arts/20150325_Edit-athon_aims_to_put_left-out_black_artists_into_Wikipedia.html.

31. Discussing racial bias on Wikipedia inferred from data about Wikimedia participants may seem like an ecological fallacy. However, the vast majority of Wikimedians are also Wikipedians. See https://stats.wikimedia.org/#/all-projects for project populations.

32. Jay Cassano, "Black History Matters, So Why Is Wikipedia Missing So Much of It?," *Fast Company*, 2015, archived at https://web.archive.org/web/20150510040813/http://www.fastcoexist.com/3041572/black-history-matters-so-why-is-wikipedia-missing-so-much-of-it.

33. Mark Muro, Sifan Liu, Jacob Whiton, and Siddharth Kulkarni, *Digitalization and the American Workforce* (Washington, DC: Brookings Institution, 2017).

34. Cf. Joseph Reagle and Lauren Rhue, "Gender Bias in Wikipedia and Britannica," *International Journal of Communication*, 5 (2011): 1139.

35. Pew Research Center, "Internet/Broadband Fact Sheet," April 7, 2021.

36. Jina Valentine and Eliza Myrie, "The Myth of the Comprehensive Historical Archive," in *Wikipedia @ 20: Stories of an Incomplete Revolution*, ed. Joseph Reagle and Jackie Koerner (Cambridge, MA: MIT Press, 2020), https://wikipedia20.pubpub.org/pub/d26b3c1u.

37. https://outreachdashboard.wmflabs.org/campaigns/black_lunch_table_2020/programs.

38. Wikipedia:Recentism.

39. Stephen Harrison, "How Wikipedia Became a Battleground for Racial Justice," *Slate*, June 9, 2020, https://slate.com/technology/2020/06/wikipedia-george-floyd-neutrality.html.

40. Talk:FUTON bias#Bias Against Books?

41. Johnny Au, "Single White Males: Systemic Bias in Wikipedia's Obsession," Wiki-pediocracy, 2015, http://wikipediocracy.com/2015/03/08/single-white-males-systemic-bias-in-wikipedias-obsessions/.

42. See, for instance, Lam, Uduwage, Dong, et al., "WP:Clubhouse?"

43. Zachary J. McDowell and Matthew A. Vetter, "It Takes a Village to Combat a Fake News Army," *Social Media + Society* (2020): 6–8, https://doi.org/10.1177/2056305120937309.

44. Zachary J. McDowell and Matthew A. Vetter, *Wikipedia and the Representation of Reality* (London, UK: Routledge, 2022), 37–40.

45. For one method of subverting this structural problem, see Matthew A. Vetter and Keon Pettiway, "Hacking Hetero/Normative Logics: Queer Feminist Media Praxis in Wikipedia," *Technoculture: An Online Journal of Technology in Society*, 7 (2017), https://tcjournal.org/vol7/hacking-hetero-normative-logics. I have also outlined a somewhat radical approach in my article "Reverting Hegemonic Ideology: Research Librarians and Information Professionals as 'Critical Editors' of Wikipedia," *College & Research Libraries* 82, no. 2 (2021): 567–83, https://doi.org/10.5860/crl.82.4.567.

46. This section is based on "Reverting Hegemonic Ideology."

47. Ira Shor, "Education Is Politics: Paulo Freire's Critical Pedagogy," in *Paulo Freire: A Critical Encounter*, ed. Peter Leonard and Peter McLaren," 32 (New York: Routledge, 1993).

48. Ira Shor, "What Is Critical Literacy?," *Journal of Pedagogy, Pluralism, and Practice* 1, no. 4 (1999): 2, https://digitalcommons.lesley.edu/jppp/vol1/iss4/2.

49. ACRL Board of Directors, *Framework for Information Literacy for Higher Education* (Chicago: Association of College and Research Libraries, 2016), 12, http://www.ala.org/acrl/standards/ilframework.

50. Shor, "Education Is Politics," 32–33.

51. Shor, "Education Is Politics."

52. Shor, "Education Is Politics," 33.

53. Paulo Freire, *Education for Critical Consciousness* (London, UK: Continuum, 2005), 21.

54. Wikipedia:Featured and good topic criteria.

55. MOS:PEACOCK.

56. MOS:WEASEL.

57. <u>MOS:LABEL</u>.
58. <u>MOS:ALLEGED</u>.
59. <u>MOS:ITSHOULDBENOTED</u>.
60. Note that the intro section (or "lead") to an article usually lacks citations, simply because this section summarizes content in the body text that has already been cited.
61. <u>Wikipedia:Citation needed</u>.
62. https://www.mediawiki.org/wiki/Who_Wrote_That%3F.
63. http://wikipedia.ramselehof.de/wikiblame.php.
64. Shor, "Education Is Politics," 32.
65. Ari Shapiro, "'There Is No Neutral': 'Nice White People' Can Still Be Complicit in a Racist Society," NPR, 2020, https://www.npr.org/2020/06/09/873375416/there-is-no-neutral-nice-white-people-can-still-be-complicit-in-a-racist-society.

Bibliography

ACRL Board of Directors. *Framework for Information Literacy for Higher Education.* Chicago: Association of College and Research Libraries, 2016. http://www.ala.org/acrl/standards/ilframework.

Au, Johnny. "Single White Males: Systemic Bias in Wikipedia's Obsession." *Wikipediocracy*, 2015. http://wikipediocracy.com/2015/03/08/single-white-males-systemic-bias-in-wikipedias-obsessions/.

Banaji, Mahzarin R., and Anthony G. Greenwald. *Blindspot: Hidden Biases of Good People.* New York: Bantam, 2016.

Barney, Stephen, W. J. Lewis, J. A. Beach, and Oliver Berghof. *The Etymologies of Isidore of Seville.* Cambridge, UK: Cambridge University Press, 2006.

Blair, Ann. "Revisiting Renaissance Encyclopaedism." In *Encyclopaedism from Antiquity to the Renaissance*, edited by Jason König and Greg Woolf, 379–97. Cambridge, UK: Cambridge University Press, 2013.

Bressen, Tree. "Consensus Decision Making." In *The Change Handbook: The Definitive Resource on Today's Best Methods for Engaging Whole Systems*, edited by Peggy Holman, Tom Devane, and Steven Cady, 212–17. San Francisco: Berrett-Koehler, 2007.

Broughton, John. *Wikipedia: The Missing Manual.* Sebastopol, CA: O'Reilly Media, 2008.

Brown, Adam R. "Wikipedia as a Data Source for Political Scientists: Accuracy and Completeness of Coverage." *PS: Political Science & Politics* 44, no. 2 (2011): 339–43. doi:10.1017/S1049096511000199.

Brown, Andrew. *A Brief History of Encyclopedias: From Pliny to Wikipedia.* London, UK: Hesperus, 2011.

Cassano, Jay. "Black History Matters, So Why Is Wikipedia Missing So Much of It?" *Fast Company*, 2015. Archived at https://web.archive.org/web/20150510040813/http://www.fastcoexist.com/3041572/black-history-matters-so-why-is-wikipedia-missing-so-much-of-it.

Cembalest, Robin. "101 Women Artists Who Got Wikipedia Pages This Week." *ARTnews*, February 6, 2014. https://www.artnews.com/art-news/news/art-and-feminism-wikipedia-editathon-creates-pages-for-women-artists-2385/.

Chozick, Amy. "Jimmy Wales Is Not an Internet Billionaire." *New York Times*, 2013. https://www.nytimes.com/2013/06/30/magazine/jimmy-wales-is-not-an-internet-billionaire.html.

Collison, Robert. *Encyclopaedias: Their History throughout the Ages.* New York: Hafner, 1964.

Creative Commons Australia. *Attributing Creative Commons Materials.* Brisbane, Australia: Australian Research Council Centre of Excellence for Creative Industries and Innovation; Creative Commons Australia, 2008.

Cummings, Robert, and Matthew Barton. *Wiki Writing: Collaborative Learning in the College Classroom*. Ann Arbor: University of Michigan Press, 2008.

Cunningham, Katie. *Accessibility Handbook: Making 508 Compliant Websites*. Beijing, China: O'Reilly, 2012.

Cunningham, Ward, and Bo Leuf. *The Wiki Way: Quick Collaboration on the Web*. Boston: Addison-Wesley, 2001.

Davis, LiAnna. *Case Studies: How Professors Are Teaching with Wikipedia*. San Francisco: Wikimedia Foundation, 2012. http://education.wikimedia.org/casestudies.

———. *Instructor Basics: How to Use Wikipedia as a Teaching Tool*. San Francisco: Wikimedia Foundation, 2012. http://education.wikimedia.org/instructorbasics.

Dillon, Michael. *Encyclopedia of Chinese History*. London, UK: Routledge, 2016.

Dodds, Felix. *Stakeholder Democracy: Represented Democracy in a Time of Fear*. London, UK: Routledge, 2019.

Doody, Aude. "Finding Facts in Pliny's Encyclopaedia: The Summarium of the *Natural History*." *Ramus* 30, no. 1 (2001): 1–22.

Duval, Jared. *Next Generation Democracy*. New York: Bloomsbury, 2010.

Eberhard, David M., Gary F. Simons, and Charles D. Fennig, eds. *Ethnologue: Languages of the World*. 22nd ed. Dallas: SIL International, 2019.

Einsohn, Amy, and Marilyn Schwartz. *The Copyeditor's Handbook: A Guide for Book Publishing and Corporate Communications*. 4th ed. Oakland: University of California Press, 2019.

Eveleth, Rose. "How Much Is Wikipedia Worth?" *Smithsonian Magazine*, October 7, 2013. https://www.smithsonianmag.com/smart-news/how-much-is-wikipedia-worth-704865/.

Freire, Paulo. *Education for Critical Consciousness*. London, UK: Continuum, 2005.

Geiger, R. Stuart, and Aaron Halfaker. "When the Levee Breaks: Without Bots, What Happens to Wikipedia's Quality Control Processes?" In *WikiSym '13: Proceedings of the 9th International Symposium on Open Collaboration*, 1–6. New York: Association for Computing Machinery, 2013.

Giles, Jim. "Internet Encyclopaedias Go Head to Head." *Nature* 438, no. 7070 (2005): 900–901. https://doi.org/10.1038/438900a.

Glott, Ruediger, Philipp Schmidt, and Rishab Ghosh. *Wikipedia Survey—Overview of Results*. United Nations University and UNU-MERIT, 2010. http://www.wikipediastudy.org/docs/Wikipedia_Overview_15March2010-FINAL.pdf.

Graham, Mark, Ralph K. Straumann, and Bernie Hogan. "Digital Divisions of Labor and Informational Magnetism: Mapping Participation in Wikipedia." *Annals of the Association of American Geographers* 105, no. 6 (2015): 1158–78.

Greenberger, Scott, Rick Holbeck, John Steele, and Thomas Dyer. "Plagiarism Due to Misunderstanding: Online Instructor Perceptions." *Journal of the Scholarship of Teaching and Learning* 16, no. 6 (2016): 72–84.

Hammer, Eric M., and Edward N. Zalta. "A Solution to the Problem of Updating Encyclopedias." *Computers and the Humanities* 31, no. 1 (1997): 47–60.

Harrison, Stephen. "How Wikipedia Became a Battleground for Racial Justice." *Slate*, June 9, 2020. https://slate.com/technology/2020/06/wikipedia-george-floyd-neutrality.html.

Ingraham, Christopher. "There Are More Museums in the U.S. Than There Are Starbucks and McDonalds—Combined." *Washington Post*, June 13, 2014. https://www

.washingtonpost.com/news/wonk/wp/2014/06/13/there-are-more-museums-in
-the-us-than-there-are-starbucks-and-mcdonalds-combined/.

Institute of Museum and Library Services. "Government Doubles Official Estimate: There Are 35,000 Active Museums in the U.S," Museum on Main Street Fact Sheet, May 19, 2014. https://www.imls.gov/news/government-doubles-official -estimate-there-are-35000-active-museums-us.

———. *Public Libraries in the United States: Fiscal Year 2016.* Washington, DC: Institute of Museum and Library Services, 2018. https://www.imls.gov/sites/default/files/ publications/documents/public-libraries-united-states-survey-fiscal-year-2016 .pdf.

Janks, Hilary. *Doing Critical Literacy: Texts and Activities for Students and Teachers.* London, UK: Routledge, 2014.

Jemielniak, Dariusz. *Common Knowledge? An Ethnography of Wikipedia.* Stanford, CA: Stanford University Press, 2014.

Kirby, Alan. *Digimodernism: How New Technologies Dismantle the Postmodern and Reconfigure Our Culture.* New York: Continuum, 2009.

Knechtges, David R. "*Huang lan* 皇覽 (Imperial Conspectus)." In *Ancient and Early Medieval Chinese Literature, Pt. 1,* edited by David R. Knechtges and Taiping Chang, 400. Leiden, Netherlands: Brill, 2010.

Kräenbring, Jona, Tika Monzon Penza, Joanna Gutmann, Susanne Muehlich, Oliver Zolk, Leszek Wojnowski, Renke Maas, Stefan Engelhardt, and Antonio Sarikas. "Accuracy and Completeness of Drug Information in Wikipedia: A Comparison with Standard Textbooks of Pharmacology." *PLOS One* 9, no. 9 (2014): 1–7. https://doi .org/10.1371/journal.pone.0106930.

Lam, Shyong K., Anuradha Uduwage, Zhenhua Dong, Shilad Sen, David R. Musicant, Loren Terveen, and John Riedl. "WP:Clubhouse? An Exploration of Wikipedia's Gender Imbalance." In *Proceedings of the 7th International Symposium on Wikis and Open Collaboration,* 1–10. New York: Association for Computing Machinery, 2011.

Lih, Andrew. "What Are Galleries, Libraries, Archives, and Museums (GLAM) to the Wikimedia Community?" In *Leveraging Wikipedia: Connecting Communities of Knowledge,* edited by Merrilee Proffitt, 7–16. Chicago: ALA Editions, 2018.

———. *The Wikipedia Revolution: How a Bunch of Nobodies Created the World's Greatest Encyclopedia.* New York: Hyperion, 2009.

Mangu-Ward, Katherine. "Wikipedia and Beyond: Jimmy Wales' Sprawling Vision." *Reason,* 2007. https://web.archive.org/web/20070814001555/https://reason .com/news/show/119689.html.

McDowell, Zachary J., and Matthew A. Vetter. "It Takes a Village to Combat a Fake News Army." *Social Media + Society* (2020): 6–8. https://doi.org/10.1177/ 2056305120937309.

———. *Wikipedia and the Representation of Reality.* London, UK: Routledge, 2022.

Melamed, Samantha. "Edit-athon Aims to Put Left-Out Black Artists into Wikipedia." *Philadelphia Inquirer,* March 24, 2015. https://www.inquirer.com/philly/ entertainment/arts/20150325_Edit-athon_aims_to_put_left-out_black_artists_ into_Wikipedia.html.

Miller, Barry X., Karl Helicher, and Teresa Berry. "I Want My Wikipedia!" *Library Journal,* 2007. https://www.libraryjournal.com/?detailStory=i-want-my-wikipedia.

Mittell, Jason. "Wikis and Participatory Fandom." In *The Participatory Cultures Handbook*, edited by Aaron Delwiche and Jennifer Jacobs Henderson. New York: Routledge, 2013.

Muhanna, Elias. *The World in a Book*. Princeton, NJ: Princeton University Press, 2019.

Muro, Mark, Sifan Liu, Jacob Whiton, and Siddharth Kulkarni. *Digitalization and the American Workforce*. Washington, DC: Brookings Institution, 2017.

Museum on Main Street Fact Sheet. "Museum on Main Street Fact Sheet." Accessed July 27, 2021. https://museumonmainstreet.org/content/faq.

Netton, Ian Richard. *Muslim Neoplatonists: An Introduction to the Thought of the Brethren of Purity*. London, UK: Routledge, 2002.

Nupedia editors. "Nupedia Newest Articles." Nupedia. Archived December 4, 2000. https://web.archive.org/web/20001204225700/http://www.nupedia.com/newest.phtml.

———. "Nupedia Newest Articles." Nupedia. Archived December 5, 2001. https://web.archive.org/web/20011205053814/http://nupedia.com/newest.phtml.

Nupedia Review Board. "Nupedia.com Editorial Policy Guidelines." Archived June 7, 2001. http://web.archive.org/web/20010607080354/www.nupedia.com/policy.shtml#approvalov.

Orlowitz, Jake. "The Wikipedia Library: The Largest Encyclopedia Needs a Digital Library and We Are Building It." In *Leveraging Wikipedia: Connecting Communities of Knowledge*, edited by Merrilee Proffitt, 69–86. Chicago: ALA Editions, 2018.

Oxford Internet Institute. *Geographically Uneven Coverage of Wikipedia*. Oxford, UK: University of Oxford, 2018. https://geography.oii.ox.ac.uk/the-geographically-uneven-coverage-of-wikipedia/.

———. *Information Imbalance: Africa on Wikipedia*. Oxford, UK: University of Oxford, 2013. https://geography.oii.ox.ac.uk/information-imbalance-africa-on-wikipedia/.

Paling, Emma. "Wikipedia's Hostility to Women." *The Atlantic*, October 21, 2015. https://www.theatlantic.com/technology/archive/2015/10/how-wikipedia-is-hostile-to-women/411619/.

Pew Research Center. "Internet/Broadband Fact Sheet." April 7, 2021. https://www.pewresearch.org/internet/fact-sheet/internet-broadband/.

Poe, Marshall. "The Hive." *The Atlantic*, 2006. https://www.theatlantic.com/magazine/archive/2006/09/the-hive/305118/?single_page=true.

Potts, Andy. "The Free-Knowledge Fundamentalist." *The Economist*, 2008. https://www.economist.com/technology-quarterly/2008/06/07/the-free-knowledge-fundamentalist.

Reagle, Joseph Michael. "Good Faith Collaboration: The Culture of Wikipedia." In *History and Foundations of Information Science*, edited by Michael Buckland and Jonathan Furner, 1138–58. Cambridge, MA: MIT Press, 2010.

Reagle, Joseph, and Lauren Rhue. "Gender Bias in Wikipedia and Britannica." *International Journal of Communication*, 5 (2011): 1138–58.

Sanger, Larry. "The Early History of Nupedia and Wikipedia: A Memoir." In *Open Sources 2.0: The Continuing Evolution*, edited by Chris DiBona, Danese Cooper, and Mark Stone, 307–38. Beijing, China: O'Reilly, 2006.

———. "Why Neutrality?" Ballotpedia, 2015. https://ballotpedia.org/Why_Neutrality.

Seigenthaler, John. "A False Wikipedia 'Biography.'" *USA Today*, 2005. http://usatoday30.usatoday.com/news/opinion/editorials/2005-11-29-wikipedia-edit_x.htm.

Shapiro, Ari. "'There Is No Neutral': 'Nice White People' Can Still Be Complicit in a Racist Society." NPR, 2020. https://www.npr.org/2020/06/09/873375416/there-is-no-neutral-nice-white-people-can-still-be-complicit-in-a-racist-society.

Sheeran, Michael J. *Beyond Majority Rule: Voteless Decisions in the Religious Society of Friends.* Philadelphia, PA: Philadelphia Yearly Meeting of the Religious Society of Friends, 1983.

Shor, Ira. "Education Is Politics: Paulo Freire's Critical Pedagogy." In *Paulo Freire: A Critical Encounter,* edited by Peter Leonard and Peter McLaren, 24–35. New York: Routledge, 1993.

———. "What Is Critical Literacy?," *Journal of Pedagogy, Pluralism, and Practice* 1, no. 4 (1999): 1–32. https://digitalcommons.lesley.edu/jppp/vol1/iss4/2.

Simonite, Tom. "The Decline of Wikipedia." *MIT Review* (2013). https://www.technologyreview.com/2013/10/22/175674/the-decline-of-wikipedia/.

Singer, Jenny. "The Women of Wikipedia Are Writing Themselves into History." *Glamour,* 2021. https://www.glamour.com/story/the-women-of-wikipedia-are-writing-themselves-into-history.

Snyder, Sara. "Edit-a-thons and Beyond." In *Leveraging Wikipedia: Connecting Communities of Knowledge,* edited by Merrilee Proffitt, 119–32. Chicago: ALA Editions, 2018.

Stothart, Chloe. "Web Threatens Learning Ethos." *The Times Higher Education Supplement,* 2012. https://www.timeshighereducation.co.uk/story.asp?sectioncode=26&storycode=209408.

Straumann, Ralph, and Mark Graham. *The Geographically Uneven Coverage of Wikipedia.* Oxford, UK: Oxford Internet Institute, 2014. https://www.oii.ox.ac.uk/news-events/news/the-geographically-uneven-coverage-of-wikipedia/.

Straumann, Ralph, Mark Graham, Bernie Hogan, and Ahmed Medhat. *Information Imbalance.* Oxford, UK: Oxford Internet Institute. https://www.ralphstraumann.ch/projects/information-imbalance-africa-on-wikipedia/.

Suler, John. "The Online Disinhibition Effect." *CyberPsychology & Behavior* 7, no. 3 (2004): 321–26. https://doi.org/10.1089/1094931041291295.

Temperton, James. "Wikipedia's World View Is Skewed by Rich, Western Voices." *Wired,* 2015. https://www.wired.co.uk/article/wikipedia-world-view-bias.

Thatcher, Jim, Michael R. Burks, Christian Heilmann, Shawn Lawton Henry, Andrew Kirkpatrick, Patrick H. Lauke, Bruce Lawson, Bob Regan, Richard Rutter, Mark Urban, and Cynthia D. Waddell. *Web Accessibility: Web Standards and Regulatory Compliance.* Berkeley, CA: Friends of ED, 2006.

Thomas, Paul A. "Reverting Hegemonic Ideology: Research Librarians and Information Professionals as 'Critical Editors' of Wikipedia." *College & Research Libraries* 82, no. 2 (2021): 567–83. https://doi.org/10.5860/crl.82.4.567.

Thomas, Paul A., M. F. Jones, and S. G. Mattingly. "Using Wikipedia to Teach Scholarly Peer Review: A Creative Approach to Open Pedagogy." *Journal of Information Literacy* 15, no. 2 (2021): 178–90. https://doi.org/10.11645/15.2.2913.

Thomas, P. L. "Power, Responsibility, and the White Men of Academia." Huffington Post, 2017. https://www.huffpost.com/entry/power-responsibility-and-the-white-men-of-academia_b_592d58bce4b08861ed0ccbce.

Tripodi, Francesca. "Ms. Categorized: Gender, Notability, and Inequality on Wikipedia." *New Media & Society* (2021): 1–21.

Valentine, Jina, and Eliza Myrie. "The Myth of the Comprehensive Historical Archive." In *Wikipedia @ 20: Stories of an Incomplete Revolution*, edited by Joseph Reagle and Jackie Koerner. Cambridge, MA: MIT Press, 2020. https://wikipedia20.pubpub.org/pub/d26b3c1u.

Vetter, Matthew A., and Keon Pettiway. "Hacking Hetero/Normative Logics: Queer Feminist Media Praxis in Wikipedia." *Technoculture: An Online Journal of Technology in Society* 7 (2017). https://tcjournal.org/vol7/hacking-hetero-normative-logics.

Wagner, Claudia, Eduardo Graells-Garrido, David Garcia, and Filippo Menczer. "Women through the Glass Ceiling: Gender Asymmetries in Wikipedia." *EPJ Data Science* 5, no. 5 (2016): 1-24.

Wells, H. G. *World Brain*. Garden City, NY: Doubleday, 1938.

Wikimedia Foundation. *Community Engagement Insights 2018 Report*. San Francisco: Wikimedia Foundation, 2018.

———. *Community Insights/Community Insights 2021 Report*. San Francisco: Wikimedia Foundation, 2021.

———. *Wikipedia Editors Study Results from the Editor Survey, April 2011*. San Francisco: Wikimedia Foundation, 2011.

———. "Wikipedia Statistics." 2019. https://stats.wikimedia.org/EN/BotActivityMatrixCreates.htm.

World Bank. "Population, Total." Accessed January 11, 2022. https://data.worldbank.org/indicator/SP.POP.TOTL?end=2019&start=2019.

Zafron, Michelle L. "Good Intentions: Providing Students with Skills to Avoid Accidental Plagiarism." *Medical Reference Services Quarterly* 31, no. 2 (2012): 225-29.

Zurndorfer, Harriet T. "The Passion to Collect, Select, and Protect: Fifteen Hundred Years of the Chinese Encyclopedia." In *Encyclopaedism from Antiquity to the Renaissance*, edited by Jason König and Greg Woolf, 505-28. Cambridge, UK: Cambridge University Press, 2013.

Index

source. *See* references
source text. *See* wikitext
source text editor. *See* wikitext
Spanish Civil War, 4
speedy deletion. *See* articles, speedy
    deletion of
Spielberg, Steven, 133
Star Wars, 1-2
"start" class. *See* articles, types of
Stinson, Alex, 119
"stub" class. *See* articles, types of
Sumer, 9
syntax highlighting, 8, 71, 86
systemic bias, 125-42; reasons for, 126,
    130-31, 132, 133; gender bias, 126-28;
    geographic bias, 128-30; racial bias,
    130-32; language bias, 128-29; ways
    to fight against, 134-43; bias towards
    digital and online resources, 132;; pop
    culture bias, 132-33
recentism, 132; "informational
    magnetism," 130

talk page, 39, 46, 81-83, 98, 103, 139-40,
    149; purpose of 46, 86; editing/
    leaving messages on, 81-83; for
    editors 46; for articles, 81; searching
    for, 46; using to defuse arguments,
    27, 31-32, 35, 98
task forces, 104, 149
templates, 63-65, 71, 83-85, 149, 158.
    See also references
"three-revert rule," 30-31
toolbar. *See* user options toolbar
translating articles. *See* articles

Uduwage, Anuradha, 126
United States, 17, 26, 28, 106-7, 110, 118,
    121, 128, 130-31
University of Alabama, 13
unregistered editors. *See* editors
Upload Wizard. *See* images
userboxes, 45
user option toolbar, 45-49, 51
user pages, 45-46, 149
user talk page. *See* talk page
usernames, 42-43, 46, 117
USSR, 1

Valentine, Jina, 131
vandalism, 27, 31, 35-36, 98-99, 139, 149
Varro, 10
verifiability, 23, 25, 90, 119, 133
visual editing, 37-68; elements of
    the visual editor, 49-50; adding
    references automatically, 56-57;
    adding references by hand, 55-56,
    57, 58; adding reference list to article,
    60-61; editing references, 59, 60;
    reusing citations, 57, 59; adding
    wikilinks, 53-54; adding external links,
    54-55; adding images to article, 61-
    62; adding section headings, 52-53;
    categorizing articles, 63; formatting
    text, 51-52; switching to/from
    wikitext editor, 49, 51; templates,
    62-65
visual editor. *See* visual editing

Wagner, Claudia, 126
Wales, Jimmy, 5, 13-18, 150
Wall Street Journal, 135
watchlist, 35-36, 39, 47-48, 67, 72, 98,
    149
"weasel words," 137, 150
"Web 2.0," 5, 16
Wei State. *See* China
Wells, H. G., 12
"Who Wrote That?" tool, 141
wiki markup. *See* wikitext
wiki technology, 16-17
WikiBlame, 141
Wikibooks, 18
WikiEducation, 117, 121-23, 161
Wikilinks, 40, 50, 53-54, 71, 75-76, 150
Wikimedia, 17, 18, 49, 61, 85, 115, 118,
    119-20, 126, 130, 150, 157n12, 162n31
Wikimedia Commons, 6, 18, 61-62, 90,
    105, 110-12, 119, 150
Wikipedia Library, 108, 119
Wikipedia Student Program, 121
Wikipedia: history of, 13-20; what it
    is not, 22-23; when to use, 4-5;
    reliability of, 19-20, 134; opposition
    to, 19-20; strengths and weaknesses
    of, 125-33; size of, 20, 125; and
    accessibility, 62, 112-14; compared

About the Author

Paul A. Thomas is a library specialist at the University of Kansas in Lawrence, as well as a PhD candidate at the Emporia State School of Library and Information Management in Emporia, Kansas. Since 2007, Thomas has been an avid Wikipedia editor who contributes to the encyclopedia under the moniker "Gen. Quon." In his many years on the site, he has created 260 articles, made more than 60,000 edits, and promoted more than 296 articles to "good" or "featured article" status. From 2017 to 2020, he also served as a Wikipedia Visiting Scholar at the University of Pennsylvania, helping to improve articles on ancient Roman and Latin literature. Thomas has written several scholarly articles about Wikipedia, which have appeared in publications such as *Transformative Works and Cultures*, *Journal of Fandom Studies*, *Journal of Information Literacy*, and *College & Research Libraries*.

CPSIA information can be obtained
at www.ICGtesting.com
Printed in the USA
BVHW041529280722
643168BV00001B/1

9 781538 163214